D0244203

SCRIBBLES IN THE MARGINS
50 ETERNAL DELIGHTS OF BOOKS

SCRIBBLES IN THE MARGINS
50 ETERNAL DELIGHTS OF BOOKS

DANIEL GRAY

B L O O M S B U R Y
LONDON · OXFORD · NEW YORK · NEW DELHI · SYDNEY

Bloomsbury Publishing
An imprint of Bloomsbury Publishing Plc

50 Bedford Square
London
WC1B 3DP
UK

1385 Broadway
New York
NY 10018
USA

www.bloomsbury.com

BLOOMSBURY and the Diana logo are trademarks of Bloomsbury Publishing Plc

First published 2017

© Daniel Gray, 2017

Daniel Gray has asserted his right under the Copyright, Designs and
Patents Act, 1988, to be identified as Author of this work.

All rights reserved. No part of this publication may be reproduced or transmitted
in any form or by any means, electronic or mechanical, including photocopying,
recording, or any information storage or retrieval system, without prior
permission in writing from the publishers.

No responsibility for loss caused to any individual or organization acting on
or refraining from action as a result of the material in this publication
can be accepted by Bloomsbury or the author.

British Library Cataloguing-in-Publication Data
A catalogue record for this book is available from the British Library.

Library of Congress Cataloguing-in-Publication data has been applied for.

ISBN: HB: 978-1-4088-8394-5
ePub: 978-1-4088-8393-8

2 4 6 8 10 9 7 5 3 1

Typeset in Haarlemmer MT by Deanta Global Publishing Services, Chennai, India
Printed and bound in Great Britain by CPI Group (UK) Ltd, Croydon CR0 4YY

Bloomsbury Publishing Plc makes every effort to ensure that the papers used in
the manufacture of our books are natural, recyclable products made from wood
grown in well-managed forests. Our manufacturing processes conform to the
environmental regulations of the country of origin.

To find out more about our authors and books visit www.bloomsbury.com.
Here you will find extracts, author interviews, details of forthcoming
events and the option to sign up for our newsletters.

To the girl who won't sleep until she's had a story.

Glasgow Life Glasgow Libraries	
L	
C 006310584	
Askews & Holts	31-May-2017
028.9	£9.99

WITHDRAWN

CONTENTS

CONTENTS

CONTENTS

CONTENTS

CONTENTS

PREFACE

OR, FINDING SOLACE IN PAGES

It is obvious and easy for an author to proclaim the many charms of books. Here, though, I am writing as a reader. This particular book is an attempt to fondly weigh up what makes a book so much more than paper and ink, how reading is so much more than a hobby, a way of passing time or a learning process. It is a celebration of the trivia that so many of us revel in, even if we don't quite realise it; an observational gallivant among impromptu bookmarks, the scents of bookshops and reading in bed.

This *Delights* book was inspired by the chance find, in a pub, of another. In J. B. Priestley's *Delight*, the author, a self-confessed 'Grumbler', toasts all that is good in the world. He is writing his way out of despondency with grim and grey post-war Britain. In short essays, we share his delight with 'Shopping in small places', 'Frightening civil servants', the 'Sound of a football', 'Sunday papers in the country', 'Smoking in a hot bath' and 109 other topics.

Priestley sought to remind his readers that there remained simple pleasures in life, no matter how dark our surroundings may seem. Now, in a cynical, jaded world of distressing news bulletins and online trolls, a world monstrously faster and angrier than Priestley's, this message is once more required. For so many of us, such sweet solace is to be found nestled among pages.

These declarations of love are about the book as a physical, almost living, object, and the rituals that surround it. They demonstrate what books and reading mean to us as individuals, and the cherished part they play in our lives from the vivid greens and purples of childhood stories to the dusty comfort novels we turn to in times of adult flux. Books are an escape door open to all people, and this one is a cosy reminder of how and why.

The long-predicted slow death of the book now seems unlikely, rendering this a good time for us to rejoice in the many and sometimes odd little ways in which the book makes us happy. Further, the place of books needs a cheerful salute, which I hope this volume is; books remain at the fulcrum of society, education and culture. They withstand and are sometimes at the forefront of technological change – ebooks are an ingenious invention and offer many joys of their own – and social trends. They still rescue many a difficult Christmas present conundrum.

Books are more attainable, and therefore democratic, than ever before. Reflecting this, these delights are, I hope, universal indulgences that are felt by the prisoner and the priest, the library-addict and the owner of a personal library. Read them, think about your own, and then move on to another book . . .

1

'To my Dear Husband. August 16th, 1936.' 'From Betty with love, Xmas '49.' 'To Sarah, keep this with you as you go. Love, Mum and Ron x.' Each of these sits snug in the top left-hand corner of an inside cover. It is almost as if the words know they shouldn't be there and are attempting to creep from the page. The handwriting is always ornately joined – 'Husband' like an unfurled and manipulated streamer from a party popper; 'Xmas' like a careful Red Arrow vapour trail – and the ink is charcoal black or early-evening blue.

The messages carried are celebratory and loving, though often in the simple and restrained language of their age. Sometimes, you sense that pen and ink liberated a book-giver not prone to spontaneous declarations of affection to go wild: 'To darling Thomas, happy birthday, Father.' There are in-jokes, too, knowing references we will never understand, and the vaguest silhouettes of lives.

Such great unknowns of book dedications are a significant part of their charm. We are transported backwards to when this book was first chosen and given, a story within the story, but this time we will never know the ending. Did Thomas enjoy the book? Did the Dear Husband even read his? Did Sarah carry hers, and to where? As so many are dated like vital contracts, we can smother these notes in their historic periods – anything written to a son between 1900 and 1914 is especially poignant – but still we are only guessing at what happened next. Did the receivers like the book, perhaps lend it to friends? How many times have these words been loved before? Was it not really the title sought after, unwrapped impatiently on Christmas Day and gladness feigned? How did it end up in the second-hand shop, or in the warehouse of the online 'used' book retailer? Had it been cherished until death and house clearance? Or passed around, through the ages, a restless minstrel yet to find home?

These paper time-machines shroud us in the comforting thought that a book has a life, and we are now a part of it. They add an extra layer of pleasure to buying an old book, and create a timeless connection between you and a long-gone reader. The two of you now share a never-to-be-revealed secret. Your lives may have been lived in very different worlds, but they are united by the exact same ink and characters.

The next time you give a book, take a moment to write a few brief words to the gift's recipient. For you are also reaching out a hand to someone who hasn't even been born yet.

2

VISITING SOMEONE'S HOME AND INSPECTING THE BOOKSHELVES

As a child, the houses I frequented had very few books on display. Most, including my home, had one or two shelves' worth, usually part of a dining-room cabinet and behind glass, as if they were to be seen and not read. Scattered in no particular order would be an abridged encyclopaedia, a bible, a dictionary, a couple of Jilly Cooper novels, some hardback photobooks about war, a set of unread plainly-bound volumes received as a gift, titles about diets and canals pertaining to midlife crises and short-lived hobbies, a tired atlas and a large annual tying in with a BBC television series.

The people who owned these shelves – my parents and my friends' parents – were born just after World War Two. When they read, books were not bought, but borrowed. Libraries were necessary and useful, whereas living-rooms were for porcelain ornaments and the telly, and not showing off. Perhaps it is why in adulthood I am fixated with bounteous shelves, and indeed with building up my own collection – we never had bookshelves, now we must have two rooms containing them. They are my pampered generation's version of indoor toilets. Or, perhaps I am just nosey.

I know that I am not alone, that there are, right now, people scanning others' bookshelves and getting to know their owners in a way conversation would not allow. These shelves are someone's biography that, try as you might to avoid it, reveal covers by which they can be judged. This isn't entirely unfair or sinister: what better way to decide if a new lover is worth wasting time on, or to find something in common with your hosts when forced into a social occasion by your more affable partner? It is also possible that those hosts *want* you to look at their shelves – a book collection can be an ostentatious display of intelligence and worldliness.

Arrival in a house or a flat kindles a desire to secure time alone with the bookshelves. The offer of a drink, preferably a slightly complicated one, is accepted, a distraction for your ferreting. Should a host be cooking, all is golden and hours are plenty.

By the time he or she is washing up, a character profile has been shaped.

Either way, there will be a rushed early scan of all shelves as you excitedly inhale the books facing you like a cat in a fish and chip shop, and pull loose two or three titles in quick succession. You might find yourself flooded with book envy, or sighing longingly at an alphabetically-organised collection of near perfection or a vast swathe of orange Penguin Classics. If there are at least half-a-dozen volumes that you too own, the omens for friendship or more are good.

A host re-enters the room to find your face illuminated having observed one such book-in-common. That is the real joy, not the prying, the searching for clues or the judging. You have found a fellow passenger and there are many worlds inside this one that you can visit together without even leaving the sofa. Best of all, when the evening's exit does come, your new friend may insist upon lending you a book or two that he or she is sure you'll love. If ever returned at all – 'It is only a fool who lends a book, and a greater fool who returns it' goes the Arabic saying – it will probably not be for a long while. When reacquainted, though, an unexpected delight is passed back to the owner.

3

IMPROMPTU BOOKMARKS

The pursuit of reading is pleasurably free of clutter. It is a simple activity, requiring no equipment or accessories, merely a book and some stolen time. Even the sole common accoutrement – the bookmark – is not necessary.

Bookmarks are the second socks of literature, frequently and inexplicably going missing in action. I have lost them all: bookmarks with tassels, bookmarks with beaded string, bookmarks boasting Shakespeare quotes, bookmarks displaying historical timelines, ribbon bookmarks, leather bookmarks and even a lavishly-designed wooden one. You could wallpaper a cathedral with the amount of card promotional bookmarks I have misplaced.

Lucky, then, that there is such delight in improvising to create makeshift bookmarks from any vaguely thin item handy. Train tickets make excellent do-it-yourself bookmarks, as do leaflets which fall from newspapers, takeaway menus, giftcards from birthday-present wrapping and even utility bills. There is also an option to 'dog-ear' the page, turning the corner into a triangle so it resembles half of a sandwich from a doll's house. This, though, violates an unspoken sanctity, scarring a book for life, as does leaving it open at the relevant pages, upside down on a bedside table, imperilling its spine and leaving fault lines. To some of us, such behaviours are acceptable and charming – a footprint and a stake claimed, or a child's height marks on a door frame never to be painted over.

All of this springs from the fear of losing your place and the need to find that place when time has finally stopped and you can read again. It is also to prevent re-reading a page or passage when there are so many other books in the world to be reading next (unfortunately, drunken reading will always mean recapping the next day). You could, of course, attempt to memorise your page number. There is theatre in trying to successfully guess it again, and turning to find that you are correct. You may even have a tiny celebration. That the rigorous march of progress is monitored in such haphazard, spontaneous a manner is a reminder that the reader is in charge. For all its regimental order, a book becomes volatile to the whims and disorder of its custodian, and blissfully temporary. Impromptu bookmarks are sandcastles built upon motorways.

4

READING IN BED

It can be the most trying of routine days. Leaking shoes, lunch made but left at home, traffic jams and interminable mid-afternoon meetings. Meetings which plunge you into an existential crisis or light sleep, meetings whose only consolation is doodling and writing down the foul made-up business-speak of senior managers. Then missed connections on the way home, absent supermarket ingredients, children who have forgotten how to sleep, rows with partners, and a packed-up boiler. Still, with every exhausting second, sanctuary ticks closer.

Lingering through daylight and evening's trials is the promise of night-time's rosy haven. You, your bed and a book: a heavenly retreat. This is double refuge – firstly, hidden from the world beneath bedcovers; secondly, entering another between book covers. Begin reading and you are transported, despite being bedridden in a day soon to close. You end it by saying goodbye and sinking into another universe. Of course, reading books should always be like this, but all is enriched in the thick quiet before midnight. The slumbering breaths of partners and children beside you are no distraction, nor rain tapping at the window or wind roaring. If anything, such comforting sounds enhance the charm of your bedtime stories. Here you are, the door is closed, the day is done, the pages are open and all the worlds you need have awoken.

Under the bedside lamp's glow, you begin one page sitting up and the next lying down. There are sideways wriggles and sighs as you struggle to find the perfect contortion for reading, and the complaints of partners awoken by laughter and gasps, but these are all part of the performance and distraction of reading in bed. Not for one line are you thinking of leaking shoes or broken boilers, and you may well be successfully putting back a dreaded tomorrow morning. Time hurtles forward – midnight comes and you recalculate the hours of sleep required. Just one more paragraph, just one more chapter, you're not ready yet for a return to reality, even if your eyelids are weighing heavier by the word. The book has become a voice whispering to you and you alone. Once more encountered is the childhood joy of reading beneath the sheets with a torch. Today is gone, tomorrow is on hold, and reading at bedtime has left you contentedly abandoned in a world all of your own.

5

BEGINNING A NEW BOOK

New books find their way to us via a number of routes. Most obvious is bricks-and-mortar store browsing. There we are, in a shop, reading the back cover, brushing fingers over embossed titles, handling and patting, appreciating the book as an object. We can tickle spines and open up to brush pages, and – if no one's looking – devour their smell. If everything chimes then the book is placed in a wrestler's headlock, claimed as a joey kangaroo in its mother's pouch. Chances are that it will soon have siblings – our eyes are bigger than our bedside tables.

Or perhaps a new book may be fostered from a library or foisted upon you by a friend who insists you will appreciate it. On the way home, blurbs are again consumed, and other furnishings idly absorbed – the review quote and the About the Author, the writer dedication and the font declaration.

Then there is that saintly thud of an online order plummeting from the letterbox, or the luscious scrape of cardboard on floor as, on returning home, you push the front door against the package. To buy online leaves you blind in comparison with bookshop scrutiny, but the gamble is surely worth the prize of feverishly setting about unwrapping the parcel. We are Charlie Bucket unwrapping a Wonka Bar, and there is a golden-ticket feeling every time.

By whichever route a book finds us, in our hands we now hold, we hope, a future escape. We are cradling delayed giggles and sobs, outcries and cheers, and flicking through pages among which we will soon find the time to lose ourselves. Before the reading begins, there is a pregnant sense of promise. The experience of this book will, if we have chosen well, enrich us and make us *feel*. It will pluck us out of the humdrum and cast us into uncertain and curious terrains, or drop us in sepia times. At this point, we do not know quite where we are going, how we will get there or indeed, whether we will even enjoy the ride. In the dawn stages of a slow-burning novel, a creeping fear can set in that this is not the book for us. Press on, though, and to find a gloopy book now motoring along by page 100 is a separate joy.

Frequently, starting a new book does not mean finishing another. There is no shame in that. In fact, it stands to emphasise just what a fine thing beginning a new book is – it is worth cheating on other titles for. It is almost impossible for us to stop ourselves: the covers are open and we are off, once more at the mercy of a new tale. It is a familiar and yet original excitement, as another journey gets underway.

6

WHEN THE LOVERS GET TOGETHER

Books make us appear to be better human beings than perhaps we are. If spotted in transit reading *Ulysses*, a stranger may think us intelligent and worldly; in reality, it is now the fifth time our eyes have waded through the same sentence on page 17. For readers there exists a generosity of emotion often lacking in real-world responses. We are capable of authentic vicarious pleasure: genuine in our happiness for the characters on a page, or heartfelt in our sorrow when catastrophe reigns. Nothing exemplifies this more than how a reader feels when two hearts collide.

This blessed moment can scatter itself across the pages in a number of ways. It can be conversational, two companions finally giving way to the hints and undercurrents that have pursued them for half a book – 'I think I'm a little bit in love with you' and 'I thought you'd never say it'. At the other extreme are wildly romantic unions, those faintly impossible eruptions and declarations of the heart involving speeches, moonlight and lavish kissing. Most of us will never experience such theatre in that moment of blending with another human, but we rarely feel jealousy as we read.

Finest of all, though, and most likely to make our hearts thump, is the coming together of our two after a long and longing pursuit – the boy sighing his way through 300 train journeys until the girl finally angles her head and smiles faintly at him. Or, the two who we *know* belong together, but seem destined to ignore our feelings, squabbling and busting-up when finally love loiters over their shoulders. Either falls into the arms of an imposter, a careless suitor. Then, something changes, truths spark and clouds break. Inside we cheer, and some of that is self-congratulatory: we knew they were meant to be together. We willed it to happen. A book's characters are not in charge of their own destiny. An author writes for us. Guiltily, we reflect that the unifications of people we actually know do not shroud us in such euphoria.

Most of all, the lovers getting together, even when they do so in a manner only possible in print or on screen, bring to us electrifying feelings last encountered years ago. They float us backwards to shaky first kisses and stomachs seasick with nerves, to buying flowers and standing outside cinemas, to late-night calls that last for hours, to being unable to think of nothing or no one other than the person who has turned up and ransacked our hearts and rationality. They remind us what it feels like to fix your hand into someone else's for the first time and find that it fits, to get goosebumps at the scent of their neck and to know nothing about someone we are falling towards, their stories still to be taken from the shelf. The reader is a benevolent voyeur, thrilled and wistful.

7

READING IN A TENT

It is possible that you haven't done this for a while, that all of your reading is undertaken beneath solid ceilings. Reading in a tent, however, is worth rediscovering, even if it means camping out in an urban garden – the curtain-twitching of neighbours adds to the sense that you are indulging in gentle disobedience.

As if to build pleasingly humdrum expectation levels, there is awkward ceremony in preparing to read in a tent. The ragtag orchestra of rustles and zips offers an avant-garde score apt for this clumsy manoeuvring. You must first contort into the tent's entrance, and steer yourself around to yank at the outside zip until it chokes shut. Then there is a crawl over discarded shoes and a cereal bowl or two into the sleeping area, followed by another graceless u-turn and a similar struggle to make metal teeth force a smile. Haul yourself into a sleeping bag without bashing your face with a knee, or crushing a family member to death, and finally, there it is – your book rests beneath your pillow, a nugget of reward.

As the sleeping bag buzzes shut around you, and that book is in your hands, a new atmosphere crackles. It falls like an interval curtain between you and the world, as if time and the moon are handing you a private space. The night belongs to you and your book. Just the two of you. And, you are reading outdoors. Not only does your book have a setting; so too do you.

Some sounds float onto your stage, welcome ballast to this seclusion: a cat fight in its devilish throes; a lone car bringing home the jaded and the drunk; a distant door slamming like the Iron Man clapping. Everything is enhanced. The type of book you are reading may help: a novel about a shipwreck or the countryside, or the autobiography of a tortured musician (but perhaps not the story of a maniac who enjoyed strangling his victims with tent rope). If the sky decides to scatter raindrops upon your tent, then you have perfection. Their pitter-patter is heavenly. Nothing could be safer or more content. You, a book and rain on the canvas. Each drop flicks the roof and slaloms as your eyes zigzag the pages. What jubilant solitude.

The torchlight fades in unison with your eyes. Your curtain is raised and to earth you must fall. Sleep visits. In the morning, a morning earlier and brighter than any other, you awake to find your book squashed in some nylon crevice, the edges of its pages curdling. It is dishevelled, as if it sneaked out to a nightclub when shut-eye reigned. Now, you must shake free from your cocoon, and embrace the daylight with one eye on the sun, and one on the clock. With the shifting of time and dropping of light can this treasured distraction happen anew.

BLOTCHES, STAINS AND OTHER REMINDERS OF WHERE AND WHEN YOU READ A BOOK

Perhaps subconsciously, you are marking your territory. The blots you leave will often be accidental, and yet they stamp authority over the book and assert that it belongs to its reader. When that book falls into your hands years later, these chance etchings are a reminder of the surroundings and era in which its words were gulped.

On page 27 of a novel, a sun-cream blotch shelters a speech mark: oh, that shabby bar in a Catalonian square, where the waitress was more beautiful than planet earth from space, where the wine was cheap and tasted cheaper, where the afternoons were born for reading with drowsy, contented eyes. On page 83 of a biography, a droplet of tea: oh, that train journey that seemed to last seven Sundays in a graveyard, the one with the damaged overhead lines near Peterborough, the one with the oversized man hemming you into your seat with elbows like pistons and shoulders broader than grey clouds over the Irish Sea, the one where only this book stood between you and criminality. Such triggers are not always so haphazard. The pages of a book are hiding places for receipts, bank advice slips, train tickets and restaurant calling cards. Perhaps they are lost bookmarks, perhaps intended keepsakes. Regardless, a book transports us elsewhere when we read it, and such items float us out of ourselves anew, perhaps into reminiscence, or a faint handshake with a time gone by. On its own, an old bus ticket is litter. Inside a book, it is a connection.

Such smears, smudges and ephemera bring a book back to you, and become a dateless, unintended diary entry. Page becomes time and place. Beside curling and scuffed leafs and bowing spines, they show how a scarred book is a loved one, a house that became a home.

9

OLD BOOKSHOPS

What joy to spot one while dawdling in an unknown place. From the opposite kerb you clock a name like Scrivener's Books and Bookbinding, Mr B's Emporium of Reading Delights or The Elliot Bay Book Company, and a busy window framed by varnished shopfronts in Scrabble-box green or wine-gum red. An imagined breeze wafts you across the road, freewill suspended, traffic and other distractions buried. You push the door, a bell rings, and you are delivered into an outpost of paradise.

There may not be a friendly greeting. Some of these shops are owned by men who were born to a higher calling than mere humanity: books. Many haven't made eye-contact with a customer for 27 years. Their postures have grown to prevent such a thing – all buckled knees and curved necks so that viewed side-on they resemble a sickle. Hunched and crouched, they scuttle around in a netherworld beneath regular sightlines, busy with grave tasks; or crumpled upon a stool, ticking and marking a list with the concentration and gravity of Noah choosing animals for the ark. That you hardly exist to him matters not. In this realm you have entered, he is one character among thousands present, and those others are begging for freedom from congested shelves.

To other proprietors that bell above the door is a sweet sound, like ice-cream van chimes or a piano outdoors. It means a new apostle has floated in, someone whose eyes will soon be saucer-wide at the view. Never are these owners pushy, and certainly they are not sales people. Such custodians of pages are there if you need them, their recommendations more astute, colourful and wilfully eccentric than any website algorithm could ever manage. They are the owners of a country mansion leaving you to enjoy the blooming gardens in your own time.

All old bookshops are united by their sacred aromas. Just as whisky develops its essence in the cask, so books mature on shelves. It is alchemy. What assails you once that doorbell chime has dimmed are instantly recognisable fragrances. There is damp, certainly, but damp with authority rather than being a cause for concern, as in a home. It is the mustiness of words fermenting. Leather, here teetering on the brink of aniseed, there of tar, hangs strong. Tobacco comes and goes as if a smoking ghost is browsing in the same sections of the shop as you. Hotchpotch carpets and rugs add spent matches. All at once you are smelling yesterday, inhaling the odours of history and feeling enormously comforted by familiarity. Open and consider a book or two and the bouquet lingers on your fingertips through an afternoon.

Subject sections in such an emporium are pleasingly chaotic, meaning it is easy to become gladly lost. 'Sport' is next to something called 'Rivers, etc'; 'Classic Novels A to M', as denoted on a yellowing sign in finest calligraphic letters, rest beside 'War and Military' (though 'Military History', as another note on slightly newer cardboard informs, 'is above

Modern History in Lower Basement'). Everything is governed by pragmatism and an antipathy to uniform furniture. 'Medicine' must joust for attention alongside 'Trains and Transportation' because both fit perfectly onto what once was the top half of a Welsh dresser. On the shelves themselves, there is order. Alphabet triumphs, though not among knee-high floor piles or batches of books stacked horizontally in front of vertical spines. These are for sorting later – tasks for the silent owner, or a satisfying Sunday distraction for the custodian in her garden.

Lost to the shelves, marooned from society with its din and streets and final clearance sales, it is possible to imagine yourself completely alone in some abandoned palace. As such, stumbling upon a fellow customer is a shock. There may be a brief smile of recognition, but silence endures. It is a reverent quiet, as if you both fear the books might take umbrage. You are left to continue your meanderings among the spines, occasionally pulling out volumes, volumes whose pencilled price marks remain in the top right-hand corner of page one, only slightly faded from the day they were left there twelve years ago.

Economic trends or other ways of buying and reading should, by rights, have slain these wonders by now. Yet the indefatigable of Durham, the unstinting of Rochester and the devoted of London are set in stone. Behind a very unchanging façade, where the kettle is always clicking or the coffee machine percolating, they are, quite by accident, tiny anarchist republics. In Durham, Rochester, London and beyond are militant cells, upholders of a variegated world from a time before so much around us resembled airport departure lounges with their terminal boredom. Most of all, though, old bookshops are as close as we bibliophiles get to walking through a wardrobe into another, living kind of nirvana.

10

HIDING YET MORE PURCHASES FROM PARTNERS

I *need* books. I feel as though I have no choice in the matter. I need shelves and stacks of them in every room in the house. Some, inevitably, will become what are termed in Japanese *tsundoku* – books bought and never read, sentenced to live forever on shelf or pile – but addiction is seldom logical.

I need to take books on holiday with me. I need to take a book on any journey I am making, whether the bus into town or a train across the country. I need to have a book or two on the go, and I need to know what I will be reading next. I need unread books on the bedside cabinet, and cherished books gone by within easy reach for checking a detail or holding fondly like an old pet brought back to life. Narcotics have nothing on this addiction. It started in a mobile library and becomes more extreme each year.

Books are my crutch. They sustain me, make me giddily happy and profoundly sad. I am never far from my next purchase, whether late at night when booze has persuaded me I must Proceed to Checkout, or in a charity shop buying a title I didn't need upon publication ten years ago, but suddenly now do. 'Is that another book?' I am asked, as I sneak upstairs, like a teenager home considerably beyond midnight or a tip-toeing cartoon burglar. As with all addicts, I have my excuses: 'It was only a fiver'; 'I haven't got this one of his'; 'I loved this when I was a kid'; and 'I had this but lent it to John and he never gave me it back'.

It is not my fault. All I am doing is giving a few hundred friends a place to stay.

11

JUST GIVING UP

Reading isn't always joyous. Sometimes, though, joy can be salvaged from the gloom.

There are occasions when a book fails to put you under its spell, when the ignition splutters and fades or the candle turns its back on the match. Your eyes move across the lines but they are shuffling rather than cantering. Words turn into bollards, sentences to blockades and paragraphs are entwined in barbed wire. To finish a chapter is to arrive flustered and late having become hopelessly lost. You revisit lines over and again, nothing much vaulting from paper to mind, and feel as if you are wading through treacle. Pages seem to be a negotiation process. The whole thing is a slog.

There are many things that can make it so: characters you don't care for, ludicrously obscure language, Latin phrases, unpunctuated sentences longer than the Golden Gate Bridge, bemusing plots and misfiring attempts at local dialects. More likely, it is a general, intangible feeling; it is bad chemistry, you and the book just don't get on. There is no anticipation, no excitement when you think about opening the book's pages while commuting or in bed. This feeling can even trigger an existential crisis – has the love gone, are reading and I *over*? To banish such thoughts, you may battle on with the book, stoic as Sisyphus.

Embedded within the reader is a feeling that to give up on a book is sacrilege, that such an act contravenes some oath or purity law, or represents a failure on your part. Worse, you are abandoning this living object, leaving a child to drown at sea. What of the poor author? You are dismissing their toil, shooing away the servant with the back of your hand. All of this is underpinned by niggling fears, reasons for persisting and blind faith in books – that this one will 'get going soon', that the plot will click, that thistly lines will begin to sing as you get used to this writer's way, that, in short, all will be well. You are governed by stubbornness and a completist's fear that a book can never be known or justifiably criticised until it has been read to the end.

Then one day, you just do it. You give up. You snap. It is a liberation. All is clear. You see that life is too short for bad books and struggling on. It is an epiphany. There is a funeral ceremony for the book: you shake your head, sigh or swear, pull away the bookmark, fan through the pages one last time, clap it shut, and take one final glance before tossing it down on the floor like an Edwardian schoolmaster dismissing an essay. Do not mourn nor feel guilty. This was a destructive relationship. You have found sweet release. There are plenty more books on the shelf.

12

READING TO A CHILD

Once upon a time and happy ever after. Dragons and beasts, fire and growls. Flawed witches and white Christmases. Girls that fly and animals that speak. Sad frogs and homespun spaceships aimed towards a moon made of cheese. What worlds to take a child to, what colour to heap upon their imagination. As you read, their heads become vivid cinemas, their hearts pounding pistons stoked by radiant fires. 'Do the voices,' they implore. 'Do the voices!' Your 'angry mother' is a triumph, your 'brazen burglar' shames seasoned actors.

Sneak a look at their eyes as you begin a new story or once more navigate a recognised one. It is as if the boulder has been rolled to reveal Aladdin's

Cave, lighting the child's face with amber rays. They inhale the pictures, colours and rhythms, and jump into the pages before them, walking among giants and ogres, giggling with chatty crows and talking to mournful oak trees.

Field all of the child's questions, give way to their interjections – stop-and-start telling does no harm. It buries a young mind even deeper in the story, it lets them drag it where they like, to become authors by the age of eight. Agree to the second story, the third and the fourth. Sleep can wait when the princess must be saved.

You, the child and a book snuggled in bed or perched on a cot-side chair, tucked away in a bedroom, everything shelter and safety. You are hidden statues rigidly in thrall to the adventures before you. The book could be newly bought or borrowed, or – a delight within a delight – one from your own youth. In such a moment, two children are united across thirty years by paper and ink.

Slowly sleep overcomes tiny eyes, the next fixture already in place: same time same place tomorrow and tomorrow's morrow. Perhaps the story runs onwards in their dreams, perhaps they blow down the house or fool the troll.

We have a few sacred years before words are unlocked and they learn to walk fairytale woods alone, that hand of yours no longer needed. You are embedding a ritual and igniting a love more intimate than any other. Tonight, you help them fly.

13

READING A TRAVEL BOOK ABOUT SOMEWHERE YOU'LL NEVER VISIT

The page is a magic carpet we can ride to distant lands. Lines of text are wings, darting us from our homes and parachuting us among igloos, forests and deserts. Travel books drop us off at Moscow Yaroslavsky in good time to catch the Trans-Siberian Express; they are paper aeroplanes braving Antarctic turbulence on our behalf. They pay no heed to borders and transplant scenes from elsewhere onto the everyday.

For a few pounds or dollars we can visit places we are curious about, but not curious enough to part with hundreds more. Better still if they are places nigh on impossible to visit – travel books smash international protocols, defy dictator decrees and etch new lines on the map. The author is a martyr, heaping troubles upon his or her shoulders so that we never need encounter them, and a courier, delivering entire continents to our doors. Airports need not be suffered, nor searing heat or glacial cold. He or she risks death in the Urals so we can know that Ukrainian rock pools harbour murky water, gobbles 17 shots of Albanian raki to inform us of its likeness to paraffin, and delivers into our nostrils the knowledge that smalltown Tunisian pillows whiff of tobacco. The writer becomes hopelessly, petrifyingly lost in a neighbourhood of staring natives and rabid stray hounds; we turn the page, gripped by the peril, elated when sanctuary is found.

This delight is enhanced if the travel book is an old one. Here, the places encountered are completely impossible to visit. Characters the author helps us shake hands and laugh with are long dead, their dialects departed and their streets folded into the ground. Perhaps even the country itself has slipped away behind war, revolution and aftermath. In this case, not only is the book allowing geographical movement – we are indulging in time travel.

Travel is permanently entertaining and occasionally exhilarating when we don't have to be there. To be taken across the world like this is to swallow a globe. Places we have never been within five thousand miles of are known intimately. We can hold a conversation about them, becoming an actor, that book a script from the vaults. A country is ticked off and then placed back on the shelf. Here is a guidebook without the hassle of identifying and being underwhelmed by recommended restaurants. We have eavesdropped on an entire nation while still lying in bed.

14

FEELING BEREFT HAVING FINISHED A BOOK

There should be a word for it – something lyrical, and probably Gaelic or ancient Greek. Only such languages could withstand the complexity involved, because the emptiness a reader encounters having completed a loved book is not one of profound sadness alone. That book has given joy that will linger and spark blissful reminiscing. There *is* a sense of loss, but also knowledge that in recent days and weeks we have been enriched by its pages. Perhaps, too, the type of person who invests so much in reading finds this soft grief not altogether uncomfortable.

This doleful pleasure works to a routine. The wedge of paper in one's right hand thins, from brick to chocolate bar to pamphlet. (What horror, incidentally, on those occasions when a fanned-flick forwards shows that what you thought were leafs of storyline are blanks or adverts for other titles; but what glee when the last page is not final, when an afterword jumps in front of the back door and greets you merrily. Endings within endings, physical twists changing book and feeling.)

Back in your hands page numbers climb, grains of sand trickling through an hourglass. The plot rises and bubbles, swirling towards satisfaction and resolution. You are simultaneously overtaken by involvement in the story (*how on earth can this end well?*) and creeping horror about real life (*no other book can ever be as good as this one*). The clock ticks towards THE END and you are lost, enraptured. Beneath the anguish, there exists a core of vindication that books still elicit this response in you, still make you feel as happy and sad, as black and white, as they did in childhood and adolescence. They remain a typeset whirlwind.

Soon, there is no more. Those characters you have spent time with – have shown patience towards, have shared moments tender, droll and wretched with, have thought (*worried*, even) about during your real life hours – are gone. Your guests have left the house.

While the book is being read, it is alive. Then it is slapped shut with a yearning sigh, and ruefully shelved. The first page giveth life, the last taketh it away. Now starts the search for something good enough to help us wallow in our bereavement all over again.

15

SCRIBBLES IN THE MARGINS

There are a protective few who see writing in a book as sinful. The very act of taking ink or lead to the page is desecration and vandalism, graffiti splattered across a sacred monument. Handwritten squiggles irritate and even offend. These delights are not all universal.

Perhaps your own views float somewhere between such militancy and complete leniency. Library books should be left alone – 'This book must be treated with care,' as school lending lists, glued to inside covers, used to read – and pens quarantined during reading. However, stumbling across gentle pencil etchings scribbled in the margins can raise the spirits like a free toy in breakfast cereals used to. Just as gifts buried deep in Ricicles meant the day started on the crest of a wave, lead markings cropping up early in a book can immediately enamour you to it. To shut them out in a fit of belligerence would be to snuff bonus life from a book.

By its nature, this pleasure springs from a pre-owned title. During an early breeze through its pages, such scribbles jump from the margin as if standing on tiptoes to be seen. They quickly transfix, leaving the printed text a few steps behind them, and may offer insight or conversely drip-feed enigma – perceptive interpretations or apparently random squiggles and words.

Scribbles take us briefly into the lives of unknown readers gone before. The fumes of revision angst and fleeting dedication to a work are trapped within. In a classic American novel, words conveying colours and textures are circled. A poetry anthology is pocked with technical terms which rest against the start of lines declaring 'simile' and 'metaphor'. Bubbly handwriting asserts that, 'He is saying here not what the line says but that his relationship with his dad is troubled.' In the pages of a play, prosaic names like Nigel and Barbara are scrawled next to 'Estragon' or 'Juliet'. Such jottings move through the years – the snooty certainties of academia, the aspiring author placing a star by impressive imagery, a lovelorn reader finding their own feelings perfectly encapsulated in one line, the tiny question marks of a grandma thriving through distance learning.

Then, the marks tail off and a book's main text is finally alone. Perhaps the pencil editor despaired and gave up, or saw nothing else worthy of action or feeling. Each scrawl, doodle and annotation is an amiable prisoner, sleeping in pages for years until released. They are dispatches from another world, adding texture and coupling readers across time. The pencil is a mighty thing.

16

LOSING AN AFTERNOON ORGANISING BOOKSHELVES

It can start with a sudden need to find a particular title, or when edging into place the recently read. Among the shelves, concentration immediately departs for another room. Books are shuffled and stroked, pulled from their berths to leave gaps in the shelf's gums, and dangerous thoughts begin: shouldn't this be over there, with his others? Surely all poetry should be together? Why are travelogues mixed in with travel guides? What *was* I thinking?

Some shifting begins. The odd errant, half-read masterpiece of a biography is retrieved from its horizontal mooring by atlases and dictionaries, turned upright, and placed among a small muster of other life stories across the room. That would be that, except your eyes have fallen upon a bygone title, which must now be grabbed and encountered. Everything is *I forgot I had this!* and *Where the hell's the sequel gone?*, the latter stirring a search. In that one act of rehousing a biography, you have become a chess piece moved around by a hundred Grand Masters of paper, ink and card.

The chain continues. Lost and found, connections made, serendipitous rediscoveries. Books are held and considered reverentially almost as if they may at any point begin to speak. Their maturing can be observed: dusty scents, amber leafs, warps and bows, and the many niggles and nobbles of advancing age. Blurbs and back covers are scanned once more, their persuasive ways charming anew, and throwing a wave back to the you that bought and read this book in times and places long ago. The typeface, chapter headings, characters, illustrations or mere feel of the object momentarily bring not only the book back to life, but the person who read it. And then you spot something else.

Time has, most likely, ceased to matter. Hours become irrelevant. Surrounding you on the floor are book piles that resemble rock formations, crumbling Roman pillars and staircases to nowhere. Deliberately or not, it appears that the shelves are being reorganised. The chaotic librarian in you proceeds. A system is concocted: half-alphabet, half-oh-that'll-fit-there; nothing too foolproof, nothing that will prevent this shambolic bliss from occurring again in a few years' time. Volumes are escorted to their new lodgings, clacking like clogs on cobbles as they land.

Finally, after this house clearance in reverse, the job is done. Now comes the moment to sit surveying your multicoloured army of straight-backed soldiers, and the moment to realise that you never did find the book you were searching for.

17

WHEN A NOVEL MAKES YOU SNIVEL

We think we're fine and then we're gone. Among the paragraphs a burn rises in the throat and holding it down with a gulp is like trying to extinguish a bonfire with a pipette. The heart rises, and then a single line momentarily tears it in two.

This is not wild bawling, and it doesn't last long. In any case, if a book has got us once, it will soon have us again. It is, in fact, controlled and measured snivelling – a shot of outward breath, a quickfire sniff or two, and at a push a sigh that comes as a surprise. Yet it retains meaning and significance, and best of all sates a reader's need for on-page sadness. As the bad news is delivered, the coffin is lowered or the justice miscarried, we can bask in luxurious melancholy and blubber at the travesty of it all.

It takes craft for an author to gather this storm, whether making a child feel deeply involved with a wronged witch, or a cynical adult become stirred by thwarted romance. That writer pulls emotion from within the reader unexpectedly, a benign hand conducting tears for their cathartic qualities. It feels good to sob, and it is difficult to forget a book that makes us do so.

There is a singular comfort in crying because of a book. It is a private outpouring of hidden emotion. It is intense and individual, and completely spontaneous, where tears in the cinema are shared and contagious. It feels easier than crying inside the real world, as if a book cover is a veil behind which repressed sensations can be aired and released.

18

NOT 'GETTING' A BOOK PEOPLE RAVE ABOUT

'Stunning,' says one jacket quote. 'An instant classic,' splashes another. Newspaper reviews gush over a month of Sundays, bestowing words such as 'masterpiece' and 'extraordinary', and cataloguing exactly why this book could well change everything we thought we knew. There on a railway station wall is its cover, swollen to barn-door size; there it is again, preening from the frazzled pages of a free newspaper discarded on a train seat. The book is talked about on the radio, and even on television. A film version, goes the rumour, is already in production. Every author's dream is coming true.

All of this can be wilfully resisted, though it is a shame not to read a book just because it has begun to behave like an invading army. What is harder to avoid is a friend's recommendation and, worse still, their foisting a copy upon you. 'It's *brilliant*,' they say, 'you'll *love* it.'

It can only be avoided for so long. Like ironing or a difficult conversation at work, it must be tackled. And so you begin. The first line jars, the second grates. The dialogue makes you wince. When your eyes scan that certain characters are about to appear, your stomach plummets as if they are making their approach in real life. You feel like ripping their names from the page. Or perhaps the writing, you acknowledge, is noble enough; it is simply the story which riles you, whether in its general bearing or because the topic is unsettling. An angry head is shaken and an incredulous thought given to its readers and devotees: what's *wrong* with these people?

Your dislike is so thorough that you can no longer suspend your disbelief, and you find yourself muttering the sacrilegious phrase, 'That would never happen.' You simply don't get it. This book is the Emperor's New Clothes but with a spin-off range of t-shirts. It makes you question first your own judgement, then the world's, and then, worst of all, your recommending friend's.

What a heretic you are . . . and isn't it wonderful? It takes courage to dissent, to risk accusations of contrariness and to prick the bubble of received wisdom. For something so small, a book can make the meekest person bold and raging. There is delight in that, and in tossing the acclaimed novel into a corner, knowing that you are right.

19

WHEN FILM AND TV ADAPTATIONS GET IT RIGHT

A novel's character strides off the page and straight into your imagination. In a flash he or she has become a physical entity, even if at first in silhouette. The character has a style of clothes, a walk, a voice – perhaps a face. Even if an author uses ample description to build a picture, much remains subject to a reader's interpretation. They score the dots and then you join them.

The same goes for a book's locations. Your brain is a set designer, cladding the walls, rolling the carpets and deciding how much casual mess to clutter the scene in. The conceiving of entire streets is left partially to you, and physical journeys are projected behind your eyes. As if to emphasise how personal such imaginings are, no two readers envisage people or places in exactly the same way. Police-style facial composites drawn from their descriptions of a character would likely turn out two very different Wanted posters.

Your perception of that character becomes sacrosanct, definitive and dear to you. Then, anxious tidings – there is to be a screen version of the book. How can whatever and whoever makes it to film match the comfort and perfection inside your head? Fears rumble, nervousness creeps: a miscast actor could usurp the finely crafted character you currently picture, ruining your mind's eye – 'that's not how he speaks'; the whole book could be badly adapted, or worse still used as mere 'source material'; you may actually have to share this story, *your story*, with millions of people. Your inclination, then, could be to avoid entirely the television or cinema adaptation. Therein sits a snobbish form of pleasure that is a cousin to *schadenfreude*.

If such petty internal squabbles can be set aside, however, a far more exuberant kind of pleasure is possible. Those tidings of a motion picture or

Sunday night series inspire excitement. Castings are announced, and, oh yes, isn't she perfect for Dickens, or isn't he an ideal Stephen King villain? There are advertisements on the television or trailers at the cinema, making your heart race. The programme is scheduled or a release date is set and anticipation turns into light-headed giddiness. It is as if the beloved book is being re-released with a fresh coating of bliss. The time comes and you demand silence in the front room, or scold the popcorn-rattler at ten paces. Your body is a tangle of butterflies and hopes. Then, the metaphorical curtain rises and with a theme tune's early notes or a first glance of a title card, exultancy springs. It is as if you are finally meeting a friend you have only ever known before via Skype or email.

A world only previously encountered on paper and inside your head is suddenly 3D, HD and Technicolor. It is like strolling into a dream. Amusements beyond the series or film itself are many. You behold characters and spot locations, comparing them with prose descriptions and your own interpretations, and reflect upon how well rendered they are. There is glee in thinking forwards to dialogue or storylines still to come, elements you cherished in print, and intrigue in wondering how they will be interpreted. Spotting nuances or identifying missing parts gives a cosy, 'insider' form of contentment.

What amasses beyond these singular, personal diversions is an overall gratification that this adaptation just feels right. The very noises it makes, the texture and colour of it, are perfect. Indeed, this version may even complement the original, its characters and worlds everything you dreamed of. Watching a childhood favourite now in screen form brings you even closer to the magic that wisped around the treasured author's typewriter.

Perhaps afterwards you remain able to separate book and adaptation, and now have a pair of versions to revel in, as if watching is like listening to a wonderful album of cover songs. The two only come together tangibly in a new edition of the book, now replete with 'As seen on TV' etchings or a fresh cover featuring a still shot from the cinema version. Or, and whisper this for it is akin to swearing in church, the adaptation, you reflect, may even be better than the book.

20

SMELLS OF BOOKS, OLD OR NEW

An hour spent inhaling books among their shelves (with the curtains closed) can summon any of the following: wet woodchips in the play-park, primary-school chairs, jumble-sale trousers, garden mud, aeroplane-cabin fumes, rubber bands, sawdust, polluted seaweed, spreadable cheese, ice-cream cones, church furniture, continental hotel rooms upon arrival, farmyards, varnish and paint in a shed, rusty batteries, a chemistry classroom, burnt toast and old two-pence coins.

Some of these scents must be worked for, some are instant. Not many are pleasant, and yet that doesn't matter; they are distinctly book odours. Any other musty item would be dismissed to the washing machine or bin. On a book, mustiness equals charm and presence.

The perfumes of the pages are wildly varied. An old hardback wears damp proudly; a new paperback is subtle and sweet. While each title's aroma is distinctive there are general scents, which is of enormous comfort to the book lover. It makes for a settling feeling, like snatching a whiff of other people's home-cooking while passing their houses. These pages may carry parts of our lives on them – the scent of a room from an old house, or a Grandad's Lambert & Butlers. They catch our throats in more ways than one.

The new book can spur strong feelings too, though this time of a less reflective, and more exultant nature. To prise open a weighty new hardback or fan through a paperback can be to expose ourselves to an infusion of bracing, fresh pages. This scent feels almost beyond description because its identity as 'new book' is so tangible in its own right, but it is closest to vinegar on fish and chips. That this comparison is with an edible, supremely evocative entity is probably no mere coincidence. The new book is tantalising and unleashes the same juices as does a favourite meal when placed down on the table in front of us.

One book can remind us of another and lead us to discovery. The picture section in a brand new autobiography's yeasty fragrance takes us instantly to the television or comic annuals we loved in our youths. Reaching for one such bygone volume, we may find the scent to have changed, now evoking an elevator just after a smoker has exited. It seems suddenly logical: of course the smell of a book changes over time. It develops and gains character, reacts to its surroundings. There appears to be no science to it – opening the exact same edition of the same novel on the same page, one copy can evoke old buses, and one Play-Doh. When all of these aromas mature and collide, a book room reaches the divine status of being identifiable as such with eyes closed. Its volumes have draped themselves across its atmosphere.

This is not a fetish. It matters because of the visceral pleasure it brings, and because it shows that books strike senses beyond just our sight.

21

FEVERISHLY AWAITING THE NEXT BOOK IN A SERIES

A curse of adulthood is the waning of anticipation. We have given up on even striving for that Christmas Eve feeling. One sacred survivor is the adult who feverishly awaits the next book in a series. They have their Christmas Eves back, perhaps even once a year.

This fever strikes young and persists. It has roots in the prolific collections, not necessarily series themselves, that make us feel assured and safe in our early years as readers. There are whole meadows of comfort when, as a pre-adolescent, one realises how many books a prolific author has written. Then, to look on library or shop shelves and see a train of similarly liveried books is to feel a hundred hugs from a book-loving father. Such certainty breeds a faith in books, and especially those titles which feel like a habit. Affinity eventually turns to wizardry obsession and queuing at midnight. This transfers seamlessly to the flutter a series brings in adulthood.

There is also now conservatism in the comfort: time is precious, risks not worth taking, we need books we will love, books that *deserve* feverish anticipation. First we hear the rumour there is to be another, then an author interview hints at news. A release date is set, previous volumes casually or seriously revisited in preparation, and pre-orders made. Future happiness and distraction has been purchased, and little chinks of Christmas Eve poke through when least expected. The thrill of the new and the comfort of the known, entwined and ours alone.

Once hooked by book one, we are embroiled and implicated. We need to know what happens next and then next again, to know how things turn out. Each time, we are reacquainting with characters, catching up and falling back into the rhythm of the book. This is a reunion, and like any reunion it can at first be awkward. Then the comfort of the recognisable begins to charm us: the story, the style and the characters; the cover, typesetting and feel. A series strikes our need for continuity and belonging, dropping us on the doormat outside our favourite front door.

Too quickly, the book is over. Then comes the satisfaction of introducing this latest recruit to the rest of its family, as if placing a further trophy in the cabinet. It is soon time to look forward to another instalment, to another Christmas Eve. Doom may one day greet the dreaded phrase 'last in the series', but deep down you know that your author can't do that to themselves, and certainly not to you.

22

HURTING WITH LAUGHTER AS YOU READ

Up it rises from the stomach. It tiptoes through the chest, tickles the throat and emerges as a wheezy splutter. Cheeks twitch, a snort escapes. It is a different kind of laughter to that which decorates shared merriment. In public and in unison, laughter is outward-facing and expressive. With a book it is personal and discreet.

This is especially true when reading in public. To stifle laughter while sitting on a bus is, joyously, the closest adulthood brings us to the impossible giggles of the classroom, those eruptions that were like fireworks in our mouths. Breathlessly, we were unable to recall what had prompted our sniggers and avoided eye-contact with our partners in crime. On that bus now, we put down our book and look away, laughing into the window.

Laughter can be plucked from any genre The odd comic image prowls among horror, and sharp dialogue pricks the pages of an intense, petrifying thriller. In those instances, mirth is relief. Where it is more frequent and consistent – the travelogue, a droll novel – laughter between us and the book becomes a cosy, extended course of in-jokes. This is private amusement, and the act of holding up the book represents a screen keeping it personal, a yawn behind the back of a hand. It is a unique form of laughter. In the pub or the cinema, or at the theatre or stand-up gig, chuckling runs to a timetable, poking a reaction from us when it sees fit. Book laughter allows us to take a joke in our own time, and interpret humour for ourselves. There is no granting of permission to laugh, only an enriching intimacy.

It is wonderful to observe a bookcase and know that among its stately spines with their shoulders back and chests forward, are slapstick, sarcasm and foul-mouthed toddlers. Such a realisation recalls the first time a stern relative is spotted mimicking a figure of authority. Within earnest pages crouch guffaws and chortles, delicious secrets waiting to make us feel helpless and teenage once again.

23

LIBRARIES

Whatever the shape and architecture of the building, a library is utopia realised. Whether stout bricks with the gentle grace of a mourner or Brutalist chamber clamped onto the side of a school this is a structure brimming with promise and nourishment. On main street corners or among tidy hidden precincts, with castle doors garnished by chiselled mottos or slender windows traced by blinds, each one of them performs the same purpose of human enrichment and sanctity.

The world indoors never differs. Devout librarians create urgency from thin air, pecking at keyboards or shuffling overdue lists, chaperoning creaky, varnished carts around and filing the returned like new mothers placing their babies in a Moses basket. They pause for fond looks at the jackets of preferred books.

Each spine with its shelf-mark code in familiar typewriter font, each date-stamp a footprint of readers gone before and each shelf with its alphabetical ordering – these things align to provide the orderliness so cherished in a library. There is safety and structure among the stacks. Everything has a place, and you have found yours.

Beyond the Romance section with its thick hard volumes by Ellas, Joannes and Paulas, and behind the audiobook and DVD racks turning gently as a lollipop lady's baton, the children's corner shimmers. What magic, for the new kid on the book and for the rest of us to look back upon and savour. It is all there: the cavernous boxes of large square books which clack when inspected by mucky fingers; worn and sagging bean bags to dwell on; laminated posters to aid counting progress; Fact Books about flags and dinosaurs; and teenage fiction with its effervescent front covers. A toddler settles himself upon his father's lap and demands to be read to. To those glancing on, it is a reminder of the majesty an early library visit possessed. Those hours were a quiet buzz, the library card a secret pass. How could it be possible to ransack a room of its books, and then carry them home and place them in yours? You didn't even get into trouble. In fact, you were *encouraged* to undertake such a task in broad daylight. Among such areas are lives mapped and shaped, their owners' hearts lost to books forever.

Upstairs in the Reference Room, amidst wooden cases and long thin drawers, amateur historians plot muddy fields on maps, and an uneasy middle-aged man studiously consults back issues of *Which?* magazine. A sleeping pensioner, here to read the newspaper, wakes himself with a nod. Back in the main library, a mum on her lunchbreak returns the kids' books late, a well-tuned smile deployed to avoid a reproachful look from the librarian; a bored lady in her seventies pops in for another crime thriller to make slow living-room clock hands dance. Earnest students find partial silence and spare plug sockets to revise and fret, and the disenfranchised use an internet simply unaffordable at home to complete job application forms.

For such a slow, hushed place, time skips along in a library, and it brims with life, whether that life crumbles or thrives. These places are havens and stimulants. Their success cannot be measured in how many times books are beeped, or in their cost per head. They are communities and refuges, growers of knowledge and vibrant democracies. Imagine closing them down for margins and savings. What ruin. Go delight in one before some twenty-first-century barbarian miser has his way.

24

LARGE BOOKSHOPS

For all that the village church feeds our soul, an occasional cathedral trip is required. We need to feel part of something wider, to be reminded that our pursuit of books and reading is neither niche nor perverse. The large bookshop reaffirms our faith, provides connection with the literary community and offers splendid opportunities to stand around reading entire chapters for free. Its floors, folds and coves are hiding places in which hours can be happily frittered away. The world turns and the high street screeches along, but Sport cushions the noise and Travel deposits you somewhere bright and quiet. There is no security guard's tap on the shoulder; after all, this *is* a bookshop.

To enter a large bookshop is to become slightly disorientated and stumble around in the dithering manner of a stunned wasp. Choice overwhelms – an unceasing corridor with wondrous doorways. The floor plan is a long-read in itself, the presence of customer lifts a further complexity. There may be a magazine section teeming with deluxe £7 works of comeliness, a whole wall of Ordnance Survey maps, and another solely dedicated to vividly coloured foreign-language dictionaries. Even the sure of mind and strong of will are weak before such decadence: we may have entered for a particular title, but then another fixes us with the glad eye and seduces its way into our home.

Such surrender and temptation are easy and they pull us across the shop, loitering in the luxury implied by twenty or thirty copies of the same volume, in handwritten staff recommendations and in three-for-two offers, where the first book is merely a gateway to the third. Tables decked out like paper picnics set another hurdle, and we are far from athletic in their presence. There is such completeness in a large bookshop, such *detail*. The answer is probably here; it is just that you have forgotten the question.

Christmas brings an invasion of hesitant brothers with titles on a list and determined grandmothers looking for 'that one by the lad in the hat off the TV'. This onslaught lends the shop a rare fizz of anxiety which enhances peacetime January all the more. The pursuit of gifts welcomes a different batch of people to our planet. As they stomp around, snatch gratefully and queue in uncomfortable radiated heat to pay, they may pluck a book for themselves and resolve to land there again, in their own time.

Outside of that season of high stress, there seems to pervade a hypnotic calm in a large bookshop. It is quite unlike the hurried atmosphere in any other high-street outlet. People dawdle and saunter rather than stride. The whole experience is so civilised that it can make us stand perfectly still, forget this troubled world and reflect to ourselves that, yes, everything is going to be all right.

25

DISCOVERING AN AUTHOR WITH A BACK CATALOGUE TO CATCH UP ON

Out there, sleeping on shelves and buried in cupboards, are favourite authors we don't yet know we love. The thought is tantalising. Fate must intervene to turn our heads in their direction – a recommendation by a friend, a written reference from another trusted writer or a chance find in a charity shop.

However the words of the previously unfound writer reach us, niggling feelings of time wasted and *Where have you been all my life?* hang on their coat-tails for a little while. Then a truth washes over us. Progressing and imbibing the first of theirs we have read, a realisation dawns that an author scarcely ever stops at one book. There may even be a list of other works within the pages of this first foray. Better still, an old title's 'also by' list will have been constructed mid-career – turns of direction and changes in pace yet to be charted. The heart soars. The end has no end. A new world beckons.

Having a list to work through adds a layer of pursuit. If an author expired some time ago, there is work to be done and thrill in the chase. Visits to second-hand bookshops now have a side mission beyond escapism, and the discovery of a chased author in the faraway nook of a charity store brings a gold-rush kick. Online trawls begin broadly but one day come to fill vital gaps – that 1938 first edition, that copy with a Foreword by George Bernard Shaw. Perhaps, to curb excess, rules are needed: no writer should be read at the exclusion of all others, so we resolve to read only our new love's pre-war fiction. It won't last, of course, but for now ours is the bounteous meadow with winter whole months away.

We order and guzzle our author's first three novels, noting the subtle shifting of styles. From this vantage, it is possible to speculate what informed such swings: did the coming of conflict lead to the darkening of this book's mood?; the finding of love sprinkle lightness upon another's? Physically, shifts in time can make your retrospective collection of editions and reissues a ragtag one when placed together, spine heights rising and falling like the crumbling turrets of an ancient fort. Cover designs fluctuate from art-deco lines of the 1930s to 1970s camp, the author's name growing in size and then shrinking again, perhaps reflecting shifts in appeal, fame and fortune. Not that this feeling is confined to yesteryear writers in starchy suits. The belated discovery of a modern author with form offers the pleasures of a past, present and future. They can be traced backwards, read until caught up with and then anticipated, which is a fresh branch to this delight. Our author may even be popular, and incite mutually admiring conversation. Perhaps, consciously or not, we have shunned her, and now can rejoice in our error.

What a thought, that there is someone out there, waiting to be discovered, and perfect for us.

26

WATCHING A CHILD LEARN TO READ

What must a toddler think as she is read to? Realms are shaped for her by black specks, loops, hooks and dots. Perhaps she imagines her reader to be a mystic bard, conjuring odysseys from the marks before them. Time slides and eyes widen. The bard becomes a codebreaker, deciphering frights, giggles and happily-ever-afters from these strange tracks.

Her reader's whispers sink in. Those eyes start to recognise parts of the code dropped elsewhere among everyday life. The 's' shapes in 'bus stop' have been discarded from a snake's hiss; on a marmalade jar are stray 'mmmms' from Goldilocks' perfect porridge. There are no boundaries between the worlds inside and outside of pages. Fantastical stories and wild creatures are melded with daily rigmarole and park swings. It would not be a surprise to the young read-to if a giant chewing on a towerblock was encountered *en route* to nursery.

Something has now stirred in the transfixed child, and a connection is made between a word and an image. It is faint and tantalising – French radio on Medium Wave or a faraway steam train – but it matters. That word 'dog' or 'car' or whatever the moment chooses is what eventually grows into a life of reading – the struck match that becomes an inferno. The child may as well have invented each noun or adjective herself, such is the joy running across her face as she reads and repeats. It is infectious, a back-to-basics rapture like someone buying you an ice cream or shouting 'echo' in a tunnel.

Soon, lines are tied together and speech marks turn from falling debris to voices. All the while, a trusty finger charts the way in fits and starts. Self-satisfied looks to parents now unfold. In turn, parents attribute significance to each moment and allow smug thoughts to cloud their brains. As they stare into a literate and literary future, the child turns on the television and shouts 'bottoms'. Still, it has started, and nothing will ever be the same again.

27

RE-READING AN OLD FAVOURITE

The circumstances are nearly always spontaneous: a lust for easy contentment, a feeble recent read that needs to be fumigated from the brain, or an eavesdropped mention of the book in question. It is rare that re-reading is planned, possibly because there is a quiet mutiny residual in this delight – it defies the thirst to proceed ever forwards in the quest of reading as many works as possible, and ignores ever-blossoming piles of newly-acquired titles.

Within those circumstances, emotional requirements may be buried. This is seldom an act pursued during a period of elation. Often, we re-read for a hug not a high-five. We have a need to return to what we know. A book which first showered consolation upon us in teenage years is a shelter during adult bouts of anxiety. Or, lonely times lead us back to a familiar character.

Teased from the shelf, the known book nestles into our hands as if coming home. Its spine is cluttered with forks of lightning and curls at the edges like haunted house wallpaper. There are tiny hackings in the cover, and varicose veins. Here is a book loved like a child's blanket or ragged teddy. Indeed, it may be a title first encountered in young days. Or perhaps a book read first a few years earlier, and then read again and differently; freed from the burden of keeping a novel's plot under surveillance, there is room to further enjoy characters, nuances and language. When not reading in earnest, new sleights of hand are detected, references understood and fragments of humour relished. The worry that a re-read will not be as good the first or ninth time most often comes to nought.

While finding new things in the old is a treat, gladness rests more in the overall sense of familiarity in which a re-read book basks. From the feel of it in one's hands, and the somehow quaint £4.50 price mark, to the author's rhythms, it gives a solid, *certain* feeling. Our life has changed, *we* have changed, but here are the same lovely words in the same perfect formations. The re-read book becomes an anchor, even if it now soothes in different ways. We are launching anew into a kindly conversation with an old teacher, and now on first name terms. Much we will have forgotten, more we will remember, but the sweeping feeling is of a return to somewhere sure.

28

WHEN THE PLOT CLICKS INTO PLACE

For a hundred pages or more, the book has opened the door and shown you around. You have met its characters and, in your head, awarded them appearances and voices. These people have taken you into their living rooms and you have escorted them around town. Their places are now recognisable – their office, their bar, their neighbourhood, their countryside. You know that the office security guard has a lisp, that the bargirl writes terrible poetry, that the family at number 18 are on a witness protection scheme, and that twenty minutes away sits heavenly countryside flanked by dark edges.

All seems clear, and yet you watch via binoculars through fog. Vigilance whisks only more murk – that lisp, bargirl, family or terrain are noted as clues for what may come, yet will likely be smokescreens. With each thickening and widening of the plot does it become harder to see straight, to imagine where this tale is heading. The author weaves the narrative with skill, churning cogs and adding layers. There are faint whispers in glances given by one character to another, but an addictive form of frustration boils within you. You may even begin to search and blame yourself – *what have I missed?* – or to hopelessly guess what is to come, a blind beggar feverishly trying to hear coins land in your pot.

The vexation this relentless building brings is absolutely necessary. It throbs the heart so that it swells in the chest, hoisting the tension until, *bang*, everything clicks into place. The relief is electrifying, the previous frustration instantly worthwhile. The killer, the mastermind, the lover or the real father is revealed and once more we breathe normally. We may 'ohhhhhhh', we may 'aaaaaahhhhh', we may swear: reading has its own compilation of pantomime sounds. The click could be cause for tears unveiled by some terrible realisation or mortal twist, more impromptu theatre after pages of intense and silent concentration. Some of that detail which has gone before now brims with meaning, much of it meant nothing, nothing beyond being happy furniture which sits so well in good stories. But now you too are in on the secret.

29

BUYING A LUXURY VOLUME THAT DOESN'T FIT ON A SHELF

It is a precious thing that extravagant, almost unfeasible, books are still produced. That they are rare, special purchases is neither here nor there. They are wallflowers that please the soul and reassure us as we pass them, gripping onto the lower reaches of bookshop ledges or stacked like flagstones in art gallery shops. When correctly executed, such volumes are a homage to photography, art, maps or musical biography.

To bend at the knees and gather one is to feel as if you are lifting a prized and precious relic. Hands move slowly and gently, white gloves are imagined into place. Covers wear textures of velvet or wallpaper unknown on smaller books, and when knuckled offer the sound of a decrepit woodpecker, while titles are resolutely engraved in warm silvers and golds. At the book's start rests a long sliver of ribbon, burrowed into the spine and adding a quiet authority as a grandfather clock's pendulum does. There are half a dozen extra pages before you may begin, as if gaining entry should be a ceremony, or a pause for expectation to grow, the gravel path trodden before entry to the grand palace. The jewels within are many and extraordinary. There are sumptuous, decorated pages whose wide spaces offer their content room not only to breathe but to beam. In the large book, images and illustrations are not supporting information; they are the headline act.

Such books can only be contemplated slowly. They are considered, rather than read. Making the leap and actually buying one is appropriately an undertaking of magnitude. There will never be a justification for purchasing a two-kilogram volume of Pop Art prints for £40, nor a 50-centimetre-tall anthology of film photography for which no plastic bag can be found. That is half the joy in taking the plunge. It is hedonistic, in book-buying terms anyway.

The large volume is somehow clutched awkwardly underneath one arm and awarded its own seat on the bus home. Its full treasures must wait until later for the fear that splaying it open now could inflict injury upon the passenger in front. Once home, the behemoth is hauled to its intended lodgings and sized against other works for shelving. It seems to shrug its shoulders and offer a customary, resigned look before you lay it on its side beneath or above the shelves.

Over the years, your luxury volume will be occasionally dabbled with – they're just *so hard to actually read* – and may grow a fading stripe where its excess leaves it vulnerable to sunlight. Knowing it is there, however, and that you are open to such wanton displays of purchasing decadence, is a lovely thing.

30

AUTHOR DEDICATIONS

When a book is opened, there is a slow gathering of momentum through its early pages. Typically, a blank page moves aside for one declaring the work's name, subtitle and author. Then comes a ladder list of 'Books by the Same Author', and italicised paragraphs of 'Praise For' this or previous works.

Turned, such decorative content gives way to earnest and weighty matters in petite fonts: first-publishing dates, second reprints and further editions; moral rights asserted and copyrights for excerpts gratefully received; stately addresses of publishing houses, CIP catalogue availability, and protracted ISBNs; chosen typefaces and typesetters, and the trustworthy names of binders and printers.

If this roll-call of the production process usually goes unread, it is with good reason – often on the facing page is the Author's Dedication, a frequently intriguing and occasionally moving detail. It may only bother the page with two or three words or a single line, yet it makes for idle moments of diverting speculation, curiosity and even sadness. Whatever the emotion stirred, a dedication nourishes the connection between author, book and reader.

What follows an innocuous word such as 'For' or 'To' offers a fragment of autobiography and conjures images. 'For my parents' usually graces an author's early books, and we see a flash of those parents, an older couple encouraging the author through exams and pretending not to be worried when she gives up her job to write a novel. 'To my darling Marie, for everything' suggests a tirelessly supportive wife, reading proofs and nursing an author's mood swings.

Anything containing initials – 'To S. R.'; 'For J. H. B.' – drips mystery onto the page, and intrigue becomes scintillating when a 'You know why' or similar is added. An in-joke between author and recipient is tantalising and we wish to be admitted to the fold. On occasion, a book is dedicated to an entire area, time period or followers of a musical genre. Perhaps it is heartfelt. Then again, perhaps the author chose no single person for fear of offending dozens more. A reader saves their longest pauses for dedications that commence 'In memory of', and souls remembered 'with deep affection'. The page becomes a time for reflection, a paper tombstone, a place where tears for someone completely unknown are justified. 'For Olivia. 20 April 1955–17 November 1962,' reads Roald Dahl's dedication in *The BFG*.

This simple concept heightens our involvement with a book before it has even begun. It is a final dose of real life and a last check of the rear view mirror before a story spirits us away. Later, we are left to daydream that one day our own name will be there, 'in deepest admiration', or, even better, as titillating initials.

31

READING IN A PUB

This is an indulgence and it is pleasure squared. To find time, room and the right pub is a rare and giddy enchantment. A charmed moment presents itself – something is cancelled, an evening while working away from home needs filling, a spare holiday hour pops up – and you escape two or three times over. Push open the pub door, and flood your eyes with both darkness and enlightenment.

Your choice of pub is critical. This spell cannot be cast in a bar where music has stepped from the background into the limelight. Neither should the pub be in a bustling, jubilant frame of mind; a smattering of ruminative denizens is ideal – any conversation should be of the idle, afternoon type. An older place with snugs and side rooms is preferable, a large chair and crackling fire greedy perfection. Cunning is needed to choose your berth. A spot behind a beam or unloved piano declares that you are not to be interrupted, that you have come to this most social of places to withdraw from humanity. You are not to be sidled up to and your wellbeing checked upon, nor engaged by the rambling bores who roam bars seeking people to detain with weather observations that turn into sprawling monologues. For illumination, dimmed lighting and even the odd candle offer enough glimmer, lending the page a treasure-map bronze.

Something about the pairing of pub and book quite simply *works*. A paperback in one hand and a pint in the other (and possibly a packet of crisps clinched between the front teeth) is earthly perfection. Those shapes fit together and feel like a prayer ritual. It may, for you, be café and book, of course, or even meal and book – there is far worse dinner company. Whatever the place and the drink, a few lines read and the first sip taken tingle together. Shoulders drop and feet uncurl like a time-lapse film of spring. A second glug and eyes galloping across lines bring a dynamic, positive fizz. Two beloved chemistries are making alchemy. Before you know it, you are deep in the story, its performance enhanced, its pages whizzing along. You are removed from time and reality until each drink ends, at which point any new and building noise must be somehow mentally swerved. There is an amble to the bar, though your imagination remains at the table and a sense of being maladjusted prevails.

Such a feeling lasts until, with the reluctance of a schoolboy traipsing home for tea, you leave and re-enter normal existence wondering when next this double refuge will beckon.

32

SPYING ON WHAT OTHERS ARE READING

Steal a sideways glance on the bus. Peep across the table on a train. Peer over your own book in the work canteen. Squint through sunglasses by the pool. Spy slyly as you pass a park bench. Gaze while idling in the café queue. Just don't get caught.

To discern what others are reading is, to some of us, impulsive. A benevolent force pulls our eyes into contact with someone else's book cover. There are certainly shades of innate literary nosiness to this, a need to snoop through the curtains. You pass judgement, too, and even feel that a stranger's choice offers an insight into their character. There will be unknown books and familiar ones. Such paperbacks in common may prompt warm thoughts of kindred spirits, perhaps even a desire to cry out, 'I've read that!', but of course you never do. Book kinship between strangers is a silent, unspoken bond. Whatever the title, there is a muffled unity between readers.

While this can often be a passing delight, in the poolside version or while occupying the tram seat behind your subject, your interest is sustained. An unintended, casual voyeurism allows you to observe how exactly others read. Their speed, progression and concentration, and the objects they employ as bookmarks make for a slow-burning, intermittent study of our species' behaviour. The way in which we read is seldom discussed; espionage like this offers tentative answers, hopefully not restraining orders.

Dearest of all are the recurring readers strafed across our routines: the middle-aged man with his spy novels on the 42 bus; at work the Polish cleaner reading more English classics than the English ever will; the split-shift waitress and her long afternoons with a detective series on a tartan blanket in the park. Such people are frequent characters in your daily stories, the choice of their next book a narrative in itself about them and about the surroundings you share. Somewhere now, the book spies and their subjects are becoming the story. Eyes mistakenly meet just above the spine, but instead of a scowl, the faintest of smiles is returned . . .

33

CHAOTIC BOOK ROOMS AND ENTHUSIASTIC OWNERS TRYING TO FIND SOMETHING FOR YOU

'I know it's here somewhere,' he bellows. His back is turned and he kneels upright, hands resting upon hips. He is seeking a particular book that came up during conversation, a throwaway remark within a digression. There is a sudden requirement for it to be located and lent to you, so here he is, looking left and right, up and down on repeat, as if wound by a key.

He sidles across to a pile behind a pile, pauses to consider a few forgotten volumes and make a mental note to revisit them, then begins working his way to the bottom, tossing away Penguin Specials and Collected Letters. The foraging must continue. Finding this book is now an obsession. From the doorway you may contend, 'It really doesn't matter. I can find it online,' but the seeker either becomes deaf or simply turns his head to dismiss the entire internet with one scathing look. A switch has been tapped, and nothing matters but finding this book, skimming through it once more and then handing it over for you to forget about.

The questing 'he' could be a vague relation or family friend most of your relatives are no longer acquainted with. It could be someone you are visiting for research purposes, or simply out of neighbourly curiosity. It can strike in any type of property, from the tiny spare bedroom to the 'library' in a Georgian mansion. Inside that book chamber shelves run against three walls at least, hinting that once, long ago, a semblance of order reigned. On top of each neat row of paperback novels are piled hardbacks, anthologies and ancient atlases. These are more recent purchases, layers added like new societies built upon older ones.

Further titles are gathered in floor stacks, loitering precariously. There could well be other objects buried beneath – papers, ornaments, furnishings, wives – but the room has succumbed to books; beautiful, disappeared books.

Then, the find. 'Got it!' or 'Told you!' or other hearty salutes. This hunched volume of probing essays, or that sallow poetry compilation, resumes its existence among us, returned from a timeless netherworld and now inserted into our life. There is resolution and harmony for him, and a celebratory hot drink is proposed. You blow the dust, sneeze and offer thanks.

34

ENTHUSING TO SOMEONE ABOUT A BOOK

Books never really end. They stay with you, good or bad, and can float into your mind quite without warning. Years later, the faint embers of a line drift across your conscience or a place you have visited only in print flickers by. The name of a character whirls around the brain like that of a primary-school classmate. Books take root. A book alters you, only in a minor way and sometimes fleetingly, but you're never completely the same when you've finished as you were on page one.

This feeling is at its rawest and most vital in the few days after you've devoured a loved book. It stalks your thoughts and prompts sighs and half-wishes that time could be reversed and our reading not yet complete. It has seeped into your consciousness, its rhythms still shadowing you. An outlet is needed, and rhapsodising to someone else helps simmer the post-book angst boiling within. It is a therapeutic post-mortem, and a chance to wildly cheer for words which until now had constituted only a private kind of joy.

The recipient of your unburdening must be chosen carefully. A friend who you think will comprehend your fervour and its cause, rather than an old man ahead of you in the supermarket queue. There must be at least some pretence that you are enthusing for their benefit, a missionary here to spread the word, armed with a copy of the good book in your hand. There is every chance your measured advocacy will lurch into nonsensical babbling, but then this is an impassioned, completely biased plea, not a critical evaluation. One 'It's just completely brilliant' rings truer than a hundred lukewarm broadsheet theses. You may misplace the plot, retell the time and make outlandish proclamations, but such is your fanaticism that when you finally draw breath, you find your listener ready to adopt the book on offer.

Your sparks have flown and now the weight of expectation sits on their shoulders – enjoy, or this friendship be damned. The need to share, though, to convert a new believer, is fulfilled.

The chain may continue, your copy passed on again and again, its corners ever more weary and dog-eared. You are left to reflect not only on the story now moored within, but on the gratifying realisation that your lust for books has not wilted with time and the seasons.

35

PRISTINE BOOKS

The new book is a slab of paradise. There are few objects as pleasing to the touch. Its textures and edges are at once both lavish and raw, and vouch for craftsmanship. Corners are tightrope-taut, covers smooth as early-morning ice rinks. A thumb dragged down a new book's fore-edge encounters a Kendal Mint Cake surface of complexity and friction. Its scent is heady and intoxicating, card and paper for now pure and unclaimed by environment.

The new book is experienced like a piece of finely carved oak, sitting flush in the hand and more natural than anything man-made should realistically be. Its spine is unperturbed by marks, pocks or thread veins, a hospital floor rather than a garden path, its hinges mousetrap-sharp. Venture inside and there rest pages in the subtle hues of moorland lambs in springtime.

None of those pages has yet to be devoured. The new book is drenched in possibility and sparkles with promise. It rests in your hands, a cheerful soul ready to lift you upon its shoulders and take you to elsewheres and never-nevers. The two of you are about to enter happy battle together. No one before you has alighted upon these words – they await your eyes, queueing in the dark until the front board is cranked open, and then sheltering themselves from the glare.

Each new book is a gift to one's self, a necessary indulgence. It is held and considered before the real diversion can begin.

36

THE BACK COVER

The back cover is consulted only after the front has been favourably judged. It hides, often with its face to the wall like a naughty schoolchild, until flipped over in someone's hands, their interest piqued. The front cover is eye-contact, the back a first conversation.

Fingers twist the book around and thumbs lock it in place, its corners nestled in our palms. Laid before our eyes is a banquet where everything is in its place, and with all the pleasing symmetries and sure features of a weather map. It offers the quiet assuredness of a childhood Sunday visit to our grandparents' house: all is where it usually is and should be; everyone is sitting in their rightful positions on furniture which seems to be bolted to the carpet.

A back cover's features are anchored and welcome. They exist, of course, to sell a book to us, yet only via the gentlest of whispered persuasions. There is often an endorsement quote from another author or a newspaper review, enthusing like a fan but never hectoring like some soap-box zealot. Two or three lines in larger fonts seek to summarise the book's contents, leaving no obligation to read onwards through a size-12 blurb, itself sprinkled with soft and friendly adjectives such as 'moving' or 'affectionate'.

Then, regular furniture rests at the cover's foot: a clinical definition of the book's genre to help booksellers – 'Cycling/Travel' directing the Saturday boy in his shelving chores; the cryptic codes and monochrome ribbons of the ISBN; prices nestled in the corner as if an afterthought, though not hidden to echo pernicious small print but murmured as if in apology that something so august as a book should be sullied by commerce; and details of a work's publishing house, not often a common language but always a steadying presence. Such markings are an identity badge and lanyard asserting a book's solid credentials without fuss. In their presence on each volume we consider reading they sate a human need for continuity and security.

The back cover may be obscured by its noisier big brother at the front, but while the latter offers lust and attraction, the former is an object of matter and substance. The two contrive to pull a reader towards a book, after which point love is entirely possible.

37

READING ON PUBLIC TRANSPORT

It may be the forty-minute plod to work, or seven hours rolling along inter-city tracks. Knees are bent and soles rested on floors two feet over urban tarmac or 10,000 above an ocean. Perched upon a liveried seat of moquette or leather, the moment has come to suspend timetables and remove the clock hands.

To open your book is to begin a retreat. Elbows are delicately arranged, place marker sought, reading matter rested on lap as if being nurtured, page spreads flattened with two knuckles, and sightlines tested and set. The human spine slaps against transport furniture and aligns with its literary brethren. In your possession is a magic wand that can whisk you away from a dreary place. Gripping and hoisting a book in front of you withdraws surroundings and leaves you in splendid isolation, in a distant world. Work colleagues may snipe about unseen managers, neighbours may barter stories of disease and death, and rowdy families may bay for attention but, as lines drift by, such distractions are swatted away. A book is both an aerial that can engage a signal received by no one else, and a Do Not Disturb sign on a hotel door handle.

Time shifts. Reading suits the rat-tat-tat rhythms of rail travel, your eyes darting along a track of their own, and the stop-start huff and puff of a bus journey, each halt and manoeuvre a paragraph outside the page. Even the sounds and jolts of an aeroplane are muffled once a book takes hold.

Your face wears a serious and yet absent expression. You have left the vehicle. Little other than daring, insolent fellow passengers with their interruptions, or the angst of travel delays and strife, can seep through and break the spell. In its own manner, so can drifting off on a warm coach, when fairytale half-sleep rolls closed resistant eyes like tinned sardine lids in reverse. A book's turns and shapes leak into slumber, fuelling perplexing dreams.

When your dull conscience whispers that you have nearly missed your stop, the book is slammed shut, thrown down and a dash back to reality begun. Already, you are looking forward to the return journey.

38

ESCAPING INTO AN ATLAS

Some types of book tip us backwards, towards innocent awe: large volumes with ornate illustrations and cross-section diagrams that show the reader 'how' and 'why'; busy almanacs of world records, conspiracies and curiosities; and compendiums of cartoon strips with their ellipses promising danger and derring-do. But most seductive of all is the atlas.

This world between covers is gathered from the shelf when it suddenly becomes important to check where Chichester is. As eyes hover over England, they rest on Eastleigh, and then pick up the sure black squiggles of a railway branch line. That line is traced along the coast to Portsmouth, Brighton and Hastings, before a hop above Norfolk, Hull and

Scarborough, each a flickering recollection of an incident, holiday, person or April afternoon, like cue cards teeing up sainted or hazy memories. To shake ourselves free and awaken elsewhere, atlas pages are shuffled and wafted onwards.

Sure lettering in the top right-hand corner announces, 'Belgium, the Netherlands and Germany'. Such two-page spreads throb with detail and intrigue, a crowd of place names jostling for position and waving for attention. Light purple borders trickle freely, resembling the backs of old men's hands, and blood-red roads dilly-dally across the page. In a City Plans section, the half-hexagon grids of Amsterdam, the prim and proper right angles of Toronto and the artful chaos of Paris sing of difference and contrary humanity. Future trips and adventures form as we look downwards and stalk our way across city and country. Some will one day turn to firm plots, dreams come true.

Onwards goes the tour of page and place. Over Murmansk or Pittsburgh, or in the hot-baked towns of Western Australia, lost in an atlas we ponder lives lived there. We picture people working, moving, kissing, striving; their existences mutually and emphatically unaware of ours, our worries or ambitions. Our fates shall never cross, but an atlas at least prompts a fanciful, longing glance. It turns us into novelists, choosing a place and conceiving a character, from the lonely cargo sailor skating along the pleasing blue of the Atlantic Ocean to the petrified climber lost among Andes mountain terracotta. Better still if yours is an old atlas, dripping with long-gone lands and old ideas, all contriving to conjure up another time in the imagination.

On fingertips we stroll across the world. The atlas allows the static mind to be broadened and opens access to secluded jungle rivers, glistening lakes and echoing airports. Its pages are laid with nourishing, unending detail that breathes into us the comfort of being part of something colossal. These are mesmeric sheets of fascination. Backwards we go.

39

MOVING IN WITH SOMEBODY AND FINDING DOUBLES

There you are, your congregations of tawny boxes lined against a barren wall. Each box varies in size, some snaffled from supermarkets, some issued by the removal company, some from the last time either of you moved. Many bow underneath heavier items, boxes with marker-pen declarations of 'kitchen stuff' caving into those branded 'towels'. Amalgamation is underway. Tin openers, toothbrush holders and washing baskets are becoming one.

When the move is complete, the door slams shut with an echoed clatter and leaves you to your mixed feelings of giddiness and terror. You slide down the wall before resting on scuffed floorboards and dusty skirting boards. An hour later, takeaway food and booze have drawn a warm veil around you. Life is fuzzy and exhilarating and bonny enough for finding music and unpacking books from boxes.

Beneath the glee there is nervousness to this process, and questions of dense matter. It may be the first time either of you has formally moved in with someone you aren't related to. Frictions lurk in shoe cupboards and sock drawers. Since books were perhaps one of the things which drew you together in the first place, introducing your collections to one another means trepidation. This is probably as close as you'll get to creating a stepfamily. How will his disturbingly comprehensive collection of railway books get on with your complete works of Thomas Hardy? Should both stocks be intermingled, or their separate identities preserved, with the added bonus of a clean, easy break should the worst happen?

The signs for your relationship are good, though, if a merger feels right. All boxes are thrown open. One by one, novels 20 centimetres high and biographies three inches fat leave their temporary shanty town in a procession. They are grouped together – his novels and yours, your non-fiction and his – and then shelved with the kind of intricacy that turns a Thursday dusk into a Friday dawn. Wonderfully, every half hour or so, one of you may exclaim 'match!', 'doubler!' or 'I've got this too!' Many you already knew of – there is just something more tangible and meaningful now these matches have met – and many you didn't. In these brief moments of pairing, it feels as though droplets of a tidy future are falling around you. Your new flat alters rapidly from carcass to cradle. All will be well and rosy.

40

GIVING A BOOK AS A PRESENT

What to buy in those frazzled moments when a gift is needed? It springs a niggling kind of fear upon the present-buyer, not least at Christmas when lists are made, broken and made again. A badly judged present is enough to prompt internal questions about a friendship or family tie. It is tantamount to casting a gypsy curse upon its recipient, even though their polite smile feigns gratitude. Choosing a book as the gift shrinks the likelihood of such a dud, and showers over the giver a feeling of serenity, as if he is some cordial monk offering quiet blessings before retreating.

Every now and again the book offered as a present has been directly mentioned, often accompanied by the words, 'But, honestly, don't bother getting me anything this year,' or taken as an inkling from a recent conversation. Beyond such direction, choosing correctly is a fine balance of science and heart, often underwritten by a check with the receiver's partner. There is a protracted bookshop visit involving the initial selection of two or three possible choices. They are then set down on a display table, finalists prodded and judged like prized cattle, and the winner selected after a period of earnest deliberation. Though there is a temptation to impose and prescribe reading matter, not always will these purchases be to your taste, as reflected in your justification of them at the till. 'That's what they all say,' offers a wary shop assistant while sliding a *True Crime Special* annual into a carrier bag.

After careful inscription and dating, the book is prepared for its new life. Wrapping it is infinitely more pleasurable than packaging other items, such are its even lines and taut corners. Three shards of Sellotape are rubbed into place making agreeable security guards, and a tag added to identify yourself with this most civilised of offerings. Following delivery, its obvious identity beneath a tree or marooned on a gift table is part of the charm: the book has no pretence or mystique, beyond the wonder of which title it could be, and is a guarantee of future blessed solitude to a birthday or Christmas-besieged recipient.

Should you witness your gift being unwrapped, the recipient's reaction will, at the very worst, be one of curiosity. It is unlikely that disappointment or disgust will rise there and then. Most likely is the consideration of your offering's title, and a quick roll over to eye its back-page credentials, before another present is dangled.

Delight in the giving is usually delayed. It rises later in the occasion when on Christmas Day late afternoon you notice the recipient filed away in a corner, flicking and beginning. Or it can bubble-up following the event – weeks after a family party, a message reaches you that 'Peter is enjoying that smashing whisky book you got him.' There is an almost selfish type of joy in becoming aware that *you* bought such pleasure, but it is bathed in the warmth of one who knows how it feels to be gifted a fitting book. For when it comes to books, receiving is the only thing greater than giving.

41

THE CALM A ROOM OF BOOKS BRINGS

Rooms full of books are not entered in a rush. The threshold of a library, pub lounge, bookshop or room in a house is breached with calm reverence, as in a place of worship. Once crossed, the book lover's pulse quickens. He or she pauses and gazes around to find they are encircled by books, before the heart slacks to the quarter peals of a village church bell. A deep and irresistible calm has arrived.

Senses are heightened. It feels as if you can hear the carpet swoosh beneath your feet, competing with pages being slid across one another and turned with a rip, a wave hissing in and smashing against the harbour wall. The wet-wood bookish scent burrows into your nose. It could be an offensive smell, and yet, because it is caused by a book's ingredients and because it is infusing a room such as this, it serves to draw you further towards tranquillity. The walls are muffled by their contents, adding to a sensation of protection, haven and retreat. No matter how many games of Cluedo you have played, nor the number of murder mysteries you have read, it feels like nothing bad could possibly happen in a room full of books.

Rather quickly for a space in which time seems denser, you lose yourself in the spines. Ageing hard-backs are most adept at drawing in this welcome displacement. Their coarse, scaly covers in steadfast greens, blues and maroons feel like the backdrop for a dream, equally alluring whether forgotten Dickens titles or botanical surveys. Fingers brush and knead them, as if magic can be dabbed and pocketed, and titles are dutifully taken down, pondered and then restored.

What sweet serenity to be encompassed by no decoration other than the words writers toiled over, to be barricaded among these entrancing objects, each with its own characters, hopes and dreams. Should the rest of the world implode, you would be just fine in this Elysian bunker.

42

PRETENDING TO HAVE READ SOMETHING YOU SHOULD HAVE

The first year of university. A shoebox cell in halls of residence. Polyester curtains that make shellsuit noises when tugged closed, and a squeaky mattress that repeats every toss and turn. In one corner, a low sink, in the other a lonely open wardrobe. The walls, cursed with slices and nicks, are all mine to populate. I do so with posters of French cinema I'll never see, bands I'm not cool enough to actually like and prints by artists I don't understand. Like half my VHS collection, CDs and books (the half on display), it is a pretence. The aim is to convey a sophisticated, appealingly aloof and charmingly troubled young man to the sequence of equally urbane women who will pass through. They never do. At least I am prepared, though.

Nearly two decades on, and the need to impress has been mostly dissolved by a mortgage and nappies. Yet there is one survivor: I still occasionally pretend to have read something I haven't. Even worse than that, I enjoy doing so.

It is usually something revered, a classic or a modern marvel. More than once, it has been a book I was told to read at school and so took umbrage with, as is a teenager's moral duty. Skeleton knowledge, scraped long ago from York Notes, helps me hold a conversation about such books, ditto watching a television adaptation or reading book reviews. Often, I own the work in question, it is just that the bookmark has not moved beyond page 32, but I get the idea.

The start of the deceit is not wholly my fault. I do not go around claiming to have read words I haven't in some dull replica of my student walls. The fraud is induced. Others begin talking and bubbling wildly about a book, my smile and brief knowledge is taken to be a deep acquaintance, and then I do not have the heart to puncture their balloon. Besides, I am by now gratified by the thrill of the lie and feel like a sharp-suited spiv, the brains behind a very mild sting. I nod along, and yes, I loved that part too. I am a budget kingpin and I am getting away with it.

Beyond the raw tingle of breaking an honest life with the gentlest of swindles, there are probably deeper reasons at play. To fake is to avoid incredulous, high-pitched reactions ('YOU'VE NEVER READ *TO KILL A MOCKINGBIRD*?!') and resultant lectures. In darker hours, it is to avoid appearing a lesser reader or to feign intellectual prowess. Mostly, though, it is the best way to avoid causing offence.

There comes a day when, finally, the great un-read and lied-about is tackled. They were right, *Huckleberry Finn* is impeccable. You just can't now say so.

43

HOTEL, B&B AND COTTAGE 'LIBRARIES'

In the life of the hotel lobby and the B&B lounge, the rented-cottage living room and apartment-block dining area, they are incidental. These small collections of books rank below corkscrews and cutlery drawers in the hierarchy of accommodation clutter, on a par with empty vases and superfluous chairs. They are extras, and rarely even the most read items in the room, flagging behind folders with plastic wallets containing Local Information, and a well-used Visitors' Book.

Still, their books remain, fluttering their covers as if by motion-sensor when guests pass. These squashed libraries are never billeted in purpose-built quarters. Their eclectic subject range is to be found stacked on pine DVD stands, former bedroom chests with the drawers removed, and neglected window sills. How these orphans arrived in holiday lodgings can only be speculated at. Some are the cottage owner's or hotel staff's surplus stock, or the holidaymaker's luggage allowance makeweight.

There is sometimes a note, begging lodgers to 'Please, take anything you like', or issuing rules such as 'Take one and leave another', or barking instructions to 'Ensure All Books Are Replaced At The End Of Your Stay. Thank You. Hotel Management'. The books are left alone in no particular order and with no discernible themes beyond 'Unwanted'. Somehow, this array offers a reading possibility for all holidaymakers, as denoted by the staple contents of such libraries: autobiographies of stand-up comedians, sportspeople and chat-show presenters; regional tour guides and maps; one *Harry Potter* volume; a later edition *Peter Rabbit* or other whole-some children's title; a thesaurus; a Ken Hom or Gordon Ramsay recipe album; a Paul Theroux or Bill Bryson travel book about somewhere else entirely; a National Geographic photography annual; and any number of works by Maeve Binchy, Frederick Forsyth, John Grisham, Danielle Steel, Harold Robbins, Stieg Larsson and Dean Koontz.

The oddity, and the deepest delight, is that somehow these books become far more attractive than whatever carefully curated choices you might have packed. They feel like bonus books; the fiver found on the pavement is far lovelier than the tenner in your wallet. The reading of one is a brief encounter. It must be devoured to the full before your stay is complete. Then, the holiday romance ends, and you return to your homely, predictable collection.

44

SQUEEZING A BOOK ONTO THE SHELF

You will never have too many books. It is impossible. Even if there is a pile in the bathroom, and some have been relegated to cardboard boxes in the loft or garage, it is still impossible. Blame your home for not having enough space, but never the books for taking up too much of it. Besides, no human ever walked into a house, flat or apartment dominated by spines and pages and found it to be soulless. Nor will this particular furnishing ever go out of fashion and be torn out or stripped back. Charity collection bags and decluttering are the enemy.

The nurture of a breathing, expanding book collection is no mean feat. At first, shelves are conventionally stacked with spines facing outwards and books in a static queue. They are simple to order, and titles easily found. As books breed, however, such cases begin to bloat. New purchases become refugees, living on the margins. They are rested horizontally across the crowns of older titles or in the small space in front of them, between book and shelf edge so that they partially peer over the edge of the cliff. Some may even be doubled up, stacked vertically so as to obscure original works, like a fresh lick of paint. In between the moment when any space on the dusty top of a bookcase has been used and a decision to begin annexing other areas of the home, there is one last resort: the squeezing in of new additions.

Once a suitable area has been identified for that addition – and it is possibly a narrow choice of berth due to an alphabetical system – a structural assessment is needed. This involves the placing of your palm on top of five or six books and the application of a shaking motion. If there is the tiniest bit of 'give', and your book is not *War and Peace*, then the squeeze is on. Prising open a gap with forefinger and thumb and then somehow holding back the tide, it becomes possible to wedge in the new arrival so that it has a foot in the door. Then, one hand is needed for further clawing against gravity to hold back whichever row, left or right, is pushing most forcibly. With the other hand, the incomer is jostled, shoved and rammed into place until just about comfortable. Any room for manoeuvre, your fingertips find upon renewed acquaintance with the book tops, has gone. This is a taut shelf. Forget reading anything from it until time and sunlight have aged loose these books' skins.

Were they to watch this caper, a book conservationist or dedicated collector would shudder. There is profound pleasure, then, in this minor act of rebellion, and in the way it allows you to refute the laws of physics. It carries the satisfaction of a job well done, DIY for the bibliophile. Any mark that is left on the squeezed book's cover, or slight limp it may possess should it try to walk, is another etching that weds you to it. This cramming-in is a display of affection – you are determined to find a home for this book, and help it settle in with others. Best of all, it creates space to grow the flock.

45

CHOOSING AND ANTICIPATING HOLIDAY READING

First, wheels or wings take you elsewhere, and then words do. Travels heaped upon travels. To pour through pages on holiday, if the right choices are made, somehow makes the reading experience thicker, the book's impact greater. In heat especially, words seem to enter your bloodstream.

Perhaps this happens because reading time is ring-fenced, and distractions plucked away one by one with each mile travelled (less so, admittedly, if you remember to pack your children). It means that the holiday book seems to have elevated status over others, and that there is extra pressure on its pages. It must perform. Though evocative and heavenly it may be, there is weight in the very phrase 'holiday

CHOOSING AND ANTICIPATING HOLIDAY READING

reading'. Beneath the veneer of contentment lurks a matter of utmost gravity. Your books represent a secondary destination, and a useful way of avoiding eye-contact with fellow holidaymakers. I have seen off Clives from Dunstable with well-turned novels and Steves from Leicester with poignant biographies. Books are shields.

The selections you make are, consequently, vital. Classically, holiday reading conjures fat thrilling paperbacks with supple spines, physically suitable for the contortions of sunbed and beach towel, and mentally so for a jaded brain shirking difficult thought. These titles must not be dismissed as 'trashy novels'; a holiday read in particular should fit the needs and tastes of its reader, the highest of which are happiness and release from everyday strife. Accordingly, burdensome tomes on American presidents or vicious battles are unfurled on holiday too. Some readers match destination to travel book, enriching their experience of a place. Reading *in situ* helps bind them to location, cultivating texture, context and a pleasing, borderline-smug veneer of regional knowledge. It means the reader has doubled-up – they are physically *and* psychologically immersed elsewhere, heightening the sense of diversion a holiday should offer.

These choices are gathered over weeks and months prior to departure. Books are 'saved' for holiday reading like an old terraced house's front room reserved for visitors, policemen or Sunday best. A holiday stash sits aloof from regular reading, which looks on, landlocked. The stash is usually wildly over-ambitious, and in many cases neglects entirely that other holiday activities such as talking to partners, daytrips and parenting will have to be undertaken. Still, when packing-time dawns, it is worth removing at least half a dozen essential items of clothing to squash into the suitcase as many books as is possible *just in case*.

A holiday's nascent hours present a chance to set the tone, to find reading places and begin filling whole days with tales from elsewhere. Those sunbeds and beach towels are portals if you can twist yourself comfortable, that cottage window-seat a chariot once you find the right angle. If a book performs its duty of absorption, all opportunities to read are snaffled – waiting for a partner to get ready or for a meal to arrive at the table, or a stolen half-hour on an apartment balcony in the heavy silence of some foreign midnight before a one-sheet bed beckons. Reading splashes itself across the holiday, becoming to your senses as integral as fresh bread and cool beer, and to your soul as vital as not being in an office.

The days roll and the date turns. Remaining time is frequently totted up, an act of self-reassurance that there is life yet in this halcyon vacation, that return flights, luggage carousels, junk mail and bad bread are still a world away: still a week to go, still four days then three, still not home until this time tomorrow, still three hours left . . . Books are forlornly repacked, the great unread among them, their pointless adventure nearly over. To look again at those you did achieve, though, is to be repaid and transported to Greece or that bewitching villa for a further fleeting second each time you glimpse their spines in passing. It can provoke a richer, more intense feeling than a photograph, such does holiday reading burrow beneath our skins.

46

LETTING POETRY TINGLE YOUR SPINE

The right lines in the right place at the right time. You could have read or heard them a thousand times over, or they may drift right through you as fresh as a spring breeze. Some poetry fixes you in its stare and invades the soul while it does so.

A poem is swallowed much more slowly than prose, as if read by the letter rather than the word. There is a need to wring a favourite verse so it, in turn, contorts the reader's insides. In one line can it grip the heart, twist the stomach and yank the tonsils. The right poem is a visceral, shuddering experience, a marked joy that sparks goosebumps the size of arrowheads, and tickles the spine with static electricity, especially if read alone and aloud.

It should be left to run without interference. Analysing the poem, dissecting it in a needless autopsy, foists science, with its ration and rules, upon a mercurial firework. It claims truths where there are none. Poetry is unquantifiable, which is why one reader's W. H. Auden is another's John Cooper Clarke. You jump upon a poem and it piggybacks you to a place of heightened senses and piercing emotions. When the last line is swallowed there is a blissful gap while you fall back to earth. For thirty seconds, you are altered, not fit for other humans and content to be that way.

A poem is yours, and cannot be experienced by anyone else quite precisely as it is by you.

47

REMEMBERING A BOOK FROM CHILDHOOD

REMEMBERING A BOOK FROM CHILDHOOD

In a furniture superstore, an overheard mother warns her child to stop swinging on a wardrobe, lest he 'end up like *Flat Stanley*'. You haven't thought of him, of that book, in twenty or more years. Immediately, you can picture its cover – the eponymous hero emerging from a musty yellow envelope dressed in a shirt and tie, in front of a wallpaper-pattern background reminiscent of a beehive. You recall how the story gave you a sense of abject fear (clearly, what happened to a little boy like Stanley Lambchop could happen to a little child like you) and of acute jealousy (how you wished that, like Stanley Lambchop, you could slide beneath doors and be a kite). You cannot remember when or where it was read to you, or if you did the reading, but the object itself and its story were woven within, obscured until now but most definitely there. While the furniture surrounding you when coming to know this story has slipped from your mind, the book's furniture has stayed. How remarkable and profound that the slightest of brushes against a memory should plunder such rich returns.

Childhood books that dwell within us are dormant and can be snapped awake by fleeting references, most joyfully in a communal setting. In a café, a book about dragons and knights is mentioned, and within minutes its perky cherry cover and the violent spikes which pierce the Lambton Worm's flesh are discussed. 'A dark, dark house' is mentioned in the workplace, and soon skeletons dancing through the night and a book jacket with butter-yellow edges are spreading warm recollections, spreadsheets abandoned. Illustrated heroes and villains lurk inside every head.

Then comes a hallowed day when a childhood book crosses from memory into possession. It may be in times sad, happy or neither; the clearing of a childhood home, the choice of the young reader you are raising, or a routine afternoon in a bookshop. When held, a silent charge pulses through the book and shrinks you backwards in time. Everything is familiar and reassuring – the feel, the cover, the drawings, the chins of the villagers, the deep-thinking cat, the peril and the end.

In the most jubilant instance this is the same copy first read, when gods and monsters first snuck into some beguiled corner of your mind. 'This Book Belongs to . . .' reads its label, and the answer is 'you', both then and now.

48

GETTING WAYLAID LOOKING AT A DICTIONARY

'I know you can be "incredulous", but can you be "credulous"? Let's see.'

Oh no, too far in: F. 'Fungo'. What a lovely word. A fungo is, apparently, '(in baseball) a ball struck high into the air for fielders to practise catching'.

You've already forgotten it though, because a few lines down 'Funicle' is winking at you. And look, 'Furfur'! 'Dandruff or scurf.' But what's 'scurf'? No, must carry on. *Credulous . . . credulous.* Skip the E pages, here are the Ds. *Credulous . . . cre—*

'Dowf'! 'Dull, heavy, spiritless.' Dowf! You really need to use that. And 'Dottle'! 'A plug of tobacco left in the bottom of a pipe.' Come on, skip the Ds, back to the Cs. *Credulous . . .*

'Daggle'! You want that word in your life. Daggle: 'to wet or grow wet by dragging or sprinkling.' Here you are, the C pages, nearly there now. Cy- . . . Cu- . . . A 'cupid' is a type of jam tart? 'Cummerbund' is a Hindi word? A 'cuddy' can be a small cabin, rent, a donkey, a stupid person or a young coalfish. What a wonderful world.

On you go, though. *Credulous* . . . Must be soon. Cry- . . . Cru- . . . 'Crunk' is a 'state of excitement' but 'crunkle' is 'to crumple'. Ha.

Nearly there. Cri- . . . Cre-. You made it. 'Creep, creel, creek, creed, cree, credulousness, credulously . . .

CREDULOUS. Credulous: 'apt to believe without sufficient evidence.' So you *can* be credulous. Oh, isn't 'credo' a . . . you're not sure quite how to describe it – a 'satisfying' word? You'll just check . . .

On it goes. A dictionary could always be your desert island book and your prison-cell must. It is an endless pursuit through which time can be squandered until a ship approaches, a sentence is served, or the maker is met. Words and meanings and origins and plurals and 64 red-striped centre pages of miscellany.

Little of the information consumed is retained, but that in itself is endearing: this wanton display of linguistic anorak behaviour has no real purpose other than momentary joy. To become wilfully lost like this is to abandon yourself to the building blocks of all your favourite books.

49

FEELING A BOOK IS INTIMATELY FOR YOU

Each book you read becomes an acquaintance. Some you look forward to seeing again, some you hide around a corner from. There are one-way friendships in which you put in all the work, and half-strangers with whom you never get beyond nodding terms – enigmatic stories that are difficult to judge. Many become frequent visitors, resting in rooms you own and occasionally being entertaining or upsetting. Then, perhaps only once a year or less, a book becomes an intimate friend.

This goes beyond simple adoration. That is certainly felt, but standing on its shoulders is a heightened level of immersion in the story. With these paragon works, you do not merely admire at arm's length: you wish to jump inside its pages. Every leaf is tickled with a detail or notion or general way of being that makes you think *this was written for me.*

This sensation can bloom when a book seems familiar, as though you are its preordained recipient. Topics, references, locations, and humour do not get under your skin, because they are already there. Here is the very embodiment of something you presently feel. A novel's characters are people, or versions of them, you have met. Each paragraph elicits empathy, each chapter ends with a knowing sigh.

Or sometimes a book can ambush you. The story may dance around remote lives and times that can never be known, but it whispers intently in your direction. It feels as though only you can truly hear its voice. As the working day forges onwards you and this title are in another dimension, awaiting the moment when you can be alone together. It is as if this book has been sent to you from some cosmic Neverland that exists to marry page and person.

Halfway through the book, it becomes inconceivable to consider that it could possibly have been written for anyone else. So tight is its grip that all reason evaporates. There may as well be a dedication to you at the start. No one can know or love this story quite so ferociously.

50

FINISHING A BOOK, PUTTING IT DOWN, AND THINKING ABOUT IT

Evening has drawn in on the book. The last lines ebb away, and then there is nothing. You look beyond The End, shifting through the plumage of any remaining pages. Endorsements for further works by this newly cherished author offer comfort, and an Acknowledgements page is clocked and will later make for an encore.

Now you dip backwards, rewinding time with a finger placed into the roulette wheels of its pages so you can pause, read a line and remember, or be reminded. With its front cover once again mulled over, the book is clapped closed and placed ceremonially on a nearby surface to lie in state. Should you be in bed, there is little chance of sleep visiting soon. Completing a book summons all-consuming thoughts of the tale now ended. They lodge in your mind like a prolonged and pealing echo.

After a while broad reflections thin to particulars. Wasn't that flawed, leading man likeable? Didn't that hospital scene strike you hard and draw tears from your eyes? The narrator's way of talking to you lingers, its prose-style, rhythms and beats still tangible. Perhaps you may even wonder what happened next to its characters.

The book's narrative overlaps with your own. There is a routine sense of emptiness and loss to flounder in during this brief gap between reads. Lurking is the danger that reality will poke through.

It won't. There is always another book to escape in.

ACKNOWLEDGEMENTS

For her love, encouragement and only occasionally complaining about the amount of books I buy, Marisa; for letting me do the voices, Kaitlyn; for wisdom and persistent support, Mark Stanton of Jenny Brown Associates; for faith in my words and always improving them, Charlotte Atyeo at Bloomsbury; for support and seeing another one over the line, Holly Jarrald at Bloomsbury.

And another tip of the flat-cap to three great Yorkshire folk: Mum, Dad and J. B. Priestley.